The Love-Tiff

Moliere

Contents

THE LOVE-TIFF

BY

Moliere

INTRODUCTORY NOTICE.

The Love-tiff (*Le Depit-amoureux*) is composed of two
pieces joined together. The first and longest is a comparatively modest
imitation of a very coarse and indecent Italian comedy,
L'Interesse, by Signer Nicolo Secchi; its intrigue depends
chiefly on the substitution of a female for a male child, a change which
forms the groundwork of many plays and novels, and of which Shakespeare
has also made use. The second and best part of the *Love-tiff*
belongs to Moliere alone, and is composed chiefly of the whole of the
first act, the first six verses of the third scene, and the whole of the
fourth scene of the second act; these, with a few alterations and a few
lines added, form, the comedy which the *Theatre Francaise* plays
at the present time. It was first represented at Beziers towards the end
of 1656, when the States General of Languedoc were assembled in that
town, and met with great success; a success which continued when it was
played in Paris at the Theatre du Petit-Bourbon in 1658. Why in some of
the former English translations of Moliere the servant Gros-Rene is
called "Gros-Renard" we are unable to understand, for both names are
thoroughly French. Mr. Ozell, in his translation, gives him the
unmistakably English, but not very euphonious name of "punch-gutted Ben,
alias Renier," whilst Foote calls him "Hugh." The incidents of
the *Love-tiff* are arranged artistically, though in the Spanish
taste; the plot is too complicated, and the ending very unnatural. But
the characters are well delineated, and fathers, lovers, mistresses, and
servants all move about amidst a complication of errors from which there

is no visible disentangling. The conversation between Valere and Ascanio in man's clothes, the mutual begging pardon of Albert and Polydore, the natural astonishment of Lucile, accused in the presence of her father, and the stratagem of Eraste to get the truth from his servants, are all described in a masterly manner, whilst the tiff between Eraste and Lucile, which gives the title to the piece, as well as their reconciliation, are considered among the best scenes of this play.

Nearly all actors in France who play either the *valets* or the *soubrettes* have attempted the parts of Gros-Rene and Marinette, and even the great tragedienne Madlle. Rachel ventured, on the 1st of July, 1844, to act Marinette, but not with much success.

Dryden has imitated, in the fourth act of *An Evening's Love*, a small part of the scene between Marinette and Eraste, the quarrelling scene between Lucile, Eraste, Marinette, and Gros-Rene, as well as in the third act of the same play, the scene between Albert and Metaphrastus. Vanbrugh has very closely followed Moliere's play in the *Mistake*, but has laid the scene in Spain. This is the principal difference I can perceive. He has paraphased the French with a spirit and ease which a mere translation can hardly ever acquire. The epilogue to his play, written by M. Motteux, a Frenchman, whom the revocation of the Edict of Nantes brought into England, is filthy in the extreme. Mr. J. King has curtailed Vanbrugh's play into an interlude, in one act, called *Lover's Quarrels*, or *Like Master Like Man*.

Another imitator of Moliere was Edward Ravenscroft, of whom Baker says in his *Biographia Dramatica*, that he was "a writer or compiler of plays, who lived in the reigns of Charles II. and his two successors." He was descended from the family of the Ravenscrofts, in Flintshire; a family, as he himself, in a dedication asserts, so ancient that when William the Conqueror came into England, one of his nobles married into it.

He was some time a member of the Middle Temple; but, looking on the dry study of the law as greatly beneath the attention of a man of genius, quitted it. He was an arrant plagiary. Dryden attacked one of his plays, **The Citizen turned Gentleman**, an imitation of Moliere's **Bourgeois-Gentilhomme**, in the Prologue to **The Assignation**.

Ravenscroft wrote "The Wrangling Lovers, or the Invisible Mistress. Acted at the Duke's Theatre, 1677. London, Printed for William Crook, at the sign of the **Green Dragon**, without **Temple-Bar**, 1677." Though the plot was partly taken from a Spanish novel, the author has been inspired by Moliere's Depit amoureux. The scene is in Toledo: Eraste is called Don Diego de Stuniga, Valere Don Gusman de Haro, "a well-bred cavaliere," Lucile is Octavia de Pimentell, and Ascanio is Elvira; Gros-Rene's name is Sanco, "vallet to Gusman, a simple pleasant fellow," and Mascarille is Ordgano, "a cunning knave;" Marinette is called Beatrice and Frosine Isabella. The English play is rather too long. Don Gusman courts Elvira veiled, whilst in the French play Ascanio, her counterpart, is believed to be a young man. There is also a brother of Donna Elvira, Don Ruis de Moncade, who is a rival of Don Diego, whilst in **le Depit-amoureux**. Valere is not the brother but the husband of Ascanio and the rival of Eraste (Don Diego) as well. The arrangement of the English comedy differs greatly from the French. Though the plot in both plays is nearly identical, yet the words and scenes in **The Wrangling Lovers** are totally different, and not so amusing. Mascarille and Gros-Rene are but faintly attempted; Marinette and Frosine only sketched in outline; and in the fifth act the ladies appear to have nothing else to do but to pop in and out of closets. The scenes of the French play between Albert and Metaphrastus (ii. 7); the very comical scene between Albert and Polydore (iii. 4) and the reconciliation scene between Lucile and Eraste (iv. 3), are also not rendered in the English comedy. There are very few scenes which can be compared with those of **le Depit amoureux**.

DRAMATIS PERSONAE.

ERASTE, *in love with Lucile*.

ALBERT, *father to Lucile*.

[This part was played by Moliere himself]

GROS-RENE, *servant to Eraste*.

VALERE, *son to Polydore*.

POLYDORE, *father to Valere*.

MASCARILLE, *servant to Valere*.

METAPHRASTUS, *a pedant*.

LA RAPIERE, *a bully*.

LUCILE, *daughter to Albert*.

ASCANIO, *Albert's daughter, in man's clothes*.

FROSINE, *confidant to Ascanio*.

MARINETTE, *maid to Lucile*.

ACT I.

SCENE I.--ERASTE, GROS-RENE.

ERAS. Shall I declare it to you? A certain secret anxiety never leaves
my mind quite at rest. Yes, whatever remarks you make about my love, to
tell you the truth, I am afraid of being deceived; or that you may be
bribed in order to favour a rival; or, at least, that you may be imposed
upon as well as myself.

GR.-RE. As for me, if you suspect me of any knavish trick, I will say,
and I trust I give no offence to your honour's love, that you wound my
honesty very unjustly, and that you show but small skill in physiognomy.
People of my bulk are not accused, thank Heaven! of being either rogues
or plotters. I scarcely need protest against the honour paid to us, but
am straightforward in every thing.

[Du Parc, the actor who played this part, was very stout;
hence the allusion in the original, "et suis homme fort rond de
toutes les manieres." I have, of course, used in the translation the
word "straightforward" ironically, and with an eye to the rotundity of
stomach of the actor. Moliere was rather fond of making allusions in his
plays to the infirmities or peculiarities of some of his actors. Thus,

in the Miser (*l'Avare*) Act I, Scene 3, he alludes to the lameness
of the actor Bejart, "Je ne me plais point a voir ce chien de
boiteux-la." "I do not like to see that lame dog;" in the Citizen
who apes the Nobleman (*le Bourgeois gentilhomme*), Act iii. sc. 9,
he even gives a portrait of his wife.]

As for my being deceived that may be; there is a better foundation for
that idea; nevertheless, I do not believe it can be easily done. I may
be a fool, but I do not see yet why you vex yourself thus. Lucile, to my
thinking, shows sufficient love for you; she sees you and talks to you,
at all times; and Valere, after all, who is the cause of your fear,
seems only to be allowed to approach her because she is compelled so to
act.

ERAS. A lover is often buoyed up by false hope. He who is best received
is not always the most beloved. The affection a woman displays is often
but a veil to cover her passion for another. Valere has lately shown too
much tranquillity for a slighted lover; and the joy or indifference he
displays at those favours, which you suppose bestowed upon me, embitters
continually their greatest charms, causes this grief, which you cannot
understand, holds my happiness in suspense, and makes it difficult for
me to trust completely anything Lucile says to me. I should feel
delighted if I saw Valere animated by a little more jealousy; his
anxiety and impatience would then reassure my heart. Do you as yourself
think it possible for any one to see a rival caressed and be as
satisfied as he is; if you do not believe it, tell me, I conjure you, if
I have not a cause to be perplexed?

GR.-RE. Perhaps he has changed his inclination, upon finding that he
sighed in vain.

ERAS. When love has been frequently repelled it frees itself, and wishes
to flee from the object it was charmed with; nor does it break its chain

so quietly as to be able to continue at peace. When once we have been fond of anyone who influenced our destiny we are never afterwards indifferent in her presence; if our dislike does not increase when we behold her our love is upon the point of returning again. Believe me, however much a passion may be extinguished, a little jealousy still dwells in our breast; no one can see, without feeling some pang, the heart he has lost possessed by another.

GR.-RE. For my part, I do not understand so much philosophy. I candidly believe what my eyes see, and am not such a mortal enemy to myself as to become melancholy without any cause. Why should I try to split hairs, and labour hard to find out reasons to be miserable? Shall I alarm myself about castles in the air? Let Lent come before we keep it! I think grief an uncomfortable thing; and, for my part, I never foster it without good and just cause. I might frequently find a hundred opportunities to become sad, but I do not want to see them. I run the same risk in love as you do; I share in your bad or good luck. The mistress cannot deceive you but the maid will do the same by me; yet I carefully avoid thinking about it. I like to believe people when they say "I love you." In order to be happy, I do not try to find out whether Mascarille tears the hair out of his head or not. Let Marinette allow herself to be kissed and caressed by Gros-Rene as much as he likes, and let my charming rival laugh at it like a fool, I will laugh too as much as I like, and follow his example; we shall then see who will laugh the heartiest.

[In several editions of Moliere we find, instead of Gros-Rene the name of Jodelet. The latest, and and if I might be permitted to say so, the most careful editor of our author, Mons. E. Despois, thinks that "Gros-Rene" ought to be mentioned here. The sense shows he is right.]

ERAS. That is like your talk.

GR.-RE. But here she comes.

SCENE II.--MARINETTE, ERASTE, GROS-RENE.

GR.-RE. Hist! Marinette.

MAR. Hallo! what are you doing there?

GR.-RE. Faith! do you ask? We were just talking about you.

MAR. Are you there too, sir? Upon my word you have made me trot about like a flunkey for this hour past.

ERAS. How so?

MAR. I have walked ten miles to look for you, and give you my word that...

ERAS. What?

MAR. That you were neither at church, in the fashionable walk, at home, nor in the market-place.

GR.-RE. You may swear to that.

ERAS. But pray, tell me who sent you?

MAR. One, in good truth, who bears you no great ill-will; in a word, my mistress.

ERAS. Ah! dear Marinette, do your words really express what she feels? Do not hide some ominous secret from me. I should not dislike you for this. For Heaven's sake tell me if your charming mistress does not merely pretend to love me?

MAR. Ha! ha! ha! What has put that funny notion into your head? Does she not sufficiently show her inclination? What further security does your love demand? What does it require?

GR.-RE. Unless Valere hangs himself, or some such trifle, he will not be reassured.

MAR. How so?

GR.-RE. He is so very jealous.

MAR. Of Valere? Ha! a pretty fancy indeed! It could only be hatched in your brain. I thought you a man of sense, and until now had a good opinion of your intellect; but I see I was very much deceived. Have you also got a touch of this distemper in your head?

GR.-RE. I jealous? Heaven forbid! and keep me from being so silly as to go and make myself lean with any such grief. Your heart guarantees your fidelity; besides, I have too good an opinion of myself to believe that any other could please you after me. Where the deuce could you find any one equal to me?

MAR. You really are right; that is as it should be. A jealous man should never show his suspicions! All that he gains by it is to do himself harm, and in this manner furthers the designs of his rival. Your distrust often is the cause that a mistress pays attention to a man, before whose merits your own have paled. I know a certain person who, were it not for the preposterous jealousy of a rival, had never been so happy as he now is. But, in any case, to show suspicion in love is acting a foolish part, and after all is to make one's-self miserable for nothing. This, sir (*to Eraste*), I mean as a hint to you.

ERAS. Very well, let us talk no more about it. What have you to say to me?

MAR. You deserve to be kept in suspense, In order to punish you, I ought to keep from you the great secret which has made me hunt for you so long. Here, read this letter, and doubt no more. Read it aloud, nobody listens.

ERAS. (*Reads*). "You told me that your love was capable of doing anything It may be crowned this very day, if you can but get my father's consent. Acquaint him with the power you have over my heart; I give you leave so to do; if his reply be favourable, I can answer for it that I shall obey." Ah I how happy am I! I ought to look upon you, the bearer of this letter, as a divine creature.

GR.-RE. I told you so. Though you do not believe it, I am seldom deceived in the things I ponder on.

ERAS. (*Reading the letter again*). "Acquaint him with the power you have over my heart; I give you leave so to do; if his reply be favourable, I can answer for it that I shall obey."

MAR. If I should tell her you are weak-minded enough to be jealous, she would immediately disown such a letter as this.

ERAS. I beseech you, conceal from her a momentary fear, for which I thought I had some slight foundation; or, if you do tell it her, say to her at the same time that I am ready to atone for my fit of madness with my life, and would die at her feet, if I have been capable of displeasing her.

MAR. Let us not talk of dying; this is no time for it.

ERAS. However, you have laid me under a great obligation; I intend shortly to acknowledge in a handsome manner the trouble so gentle and so lovely a messenger has taken.

MAR. That reminds me. Do you know where I looked for you just now?

ERAS. Well?

MAR. Quite near the market-place; you know where that is.

ERAS. Where did you say?

MAR. There... in that shop where last month you generously and freely promised me a ring.

ERAS. Um! I understand you.

GR.-RE. What a cunning jade!

ERAS. It is true; I have delayed too long to make good my promise to you, but...

MAR. What I said, sir, was not because I wished you to make haste.

GR.-RE. Oh, no!

ERAS. (*Giving her his ring*). Perhaps this ring may please you; accept it instead of the one I owe.

MAR. You are only jesting, sir; I should be ashamed to take it.

GR.-RE. Poor shame-faced creature! Take it without more ado; only fools refuse what is offered them.

MAR. I will only accept it so that I may have something to remember you by.

ERAS. When may I return thanks to that lovely angel?

MAR. Endeavour to gain over her father.

ERAS. But if he rejects me, should I...?

MAR. We will think about that when he does so! We will do our utmost for you: one way or another she must be yours; do your best, and we will do ours.

ERAS. Farewell! we shall know our fate to-day. (Eraste reads the letter again to himself).

MAR. (*To Gros-Rene*). Well, what shall we say of our love? You do not speak to me of it.

GR.-RE. If such people as we wish to be married, the thing is soon done. I will have you. Will you have me?

MAR. Gladly.

GR.-RE. Shake hands, that is enough.

MAR. Farewell, Gros-Rene, my heart's delight.

GR.-RE. Farewell, my star.

MAR. Farewell, fair fire-brand of my flame.

GR.-RE. Farewell, dear comet, rainbow of my soul. (Exit Marinette). Heaven be praised, our affairs go on swimmingly. Albert is not a man to refuse you anything.

ERAS. Valere is coming here.

GR.-RE. I pity the poor wretch, knowing what I do know.

SCENE III.--ERASTE, VALERE, GROS-RENE.

ERAS. Well, Valere?

VAL. Well, Eraste?

ERAS. How does your love prosper?

VAL. And how does yours?

ERAS. It grows stronger and stronger every day.

VAL. So does mine.

ERAS. For Lucile?

VAL. For her.

ERAS. Certainly, I must own, you are a pattern of uncommon constancy.

VAL. And your perseverance will be a rare example to posterity.

ERAS. As for me, I am not very fond of that austere kind of love which is satisfied with looks only; nor do I possess feelings lofty enough to endure ill-treatment with constancy. In one word, when I really love, I wish to be beloved again.

VAL. It is very natural, and I am of the same opinion. I would never do homage to the most perfect object by whom I could be smitten, if she did not return my passion.

ERAS. However, Lucile...

VAL. Lucile does willingly everything my passion can desire.

ERAS. You are easily satisfied then.

VAL. Not so easily as you may think.

ERAS. I, however, may, without vanity, believe that I am in her favour.

VAL. And I know that I have a very good share of it.

ERAS. Do not deceive yourself; believe me.

VAL. Believe me, do not be too credulous, and take too much for granted.

ERAS. If I might show you a certain proof that her heart...but no, it would too much distress you.

VAL. If I might discover a secret to you...but it might grieve you, and so I will be discreet.

ERAS. You really urge me too far, and though much against my will, I see I must lower your presumption. Read that.

VAL. (***After having read the letter***). These are tender words.

ERAS. You know the handwriting?

VAL. Yes, it is Lucile's.

ERAS. Well! where is now your boasted certainty...?

VAL. (***Smiling and going away***). Farewell, Eraste.

GR.-RE. He is mad, surely. What reason has he to laugh?

ERAS. He certainly surprises me, and between ourselves I cannot imagine what the deuce of a mystery is hidden under this.

GR.-RE. Here comes his servant, I think.

ERAS. Yes, it is he; let us play the hypocrite, to set him talking about his master's love.

SCENE IV.--ERASTE, MASCARILLE, GROS-RENE.

MASC. (*Aside*). No, I do not know a more wretched situation, than to have a young master, very much in love.

GR.-RE. Good morning.

MASC. Good morning.

GR.-RE. Where is Mascarille going just now? What is he doing? Is he coming back? Is he going away? Or does he intend to stay where he is?

MASC. No, I am not coming back, because I have not yet been where I am going; nor am I going, for I am stopped; nor do I design to stay, for this very moment I intend to be gone.

ERAS. You are very abrupt, Mascarille; gently.

MASC. Ha! Your servant, sir.

ERAS. You are in great haste to run away from us: what! do I frighten you?

MASC. You are too courteous to do that.

ERAS. Shake hands; all jealousy is now at an end between us; we will be friends; I have relinquished my love; henceforth you can have your own way to further your happiness.

MASC. Would to Heaven it were true!

ERAS. Gros-Rene knows that I have already another flame elsewhere.

GR.-RE. Certainly; and I also give up Marinette to you.

MASC. Do not let us touch on that point; our rivalry is not likely to go to such a length. But is it certain, sir, that you are no longer in love, or do you jest?

ERAS. I have been informed that your master is but too fortunate in his amours; I should be a fool to pretend any longer to gain the same favours which that lady grants to him alone.

MASC. Certainly, you please me with this news. Though I was rather afraid of you, with regard to our plans, yet you do wisely to slip your neck out of the collar. You have done well to leave a house where you were only caressed for form's sake; I, knowing all that was going on, have many times pitied you, because you were allured by expectations, which could never be realized. It is a sin and a shame to deceive a gentleman! But how the deuce, after all, did you find out the trick? For when they plighted their faith to each other there were no witnesses but night, myself, and two others; and the tying of the knot, which satisfies the passion of our lovers, is thought to have been kept a secret till now.

ERAS. Ha! What do you say?

MASC. I say that I am amazed, sir, and cannot guess who told you, that under this mask, which deceives you and everybody else, a secret marriage unites their matchless love.

ERAS. You lie.

MASC. Sir, with all my heart.

ERAS. You are a rascal.

MASC. I acknowledge I am.

ERAS. And this impudence deserves a sound beating on the spot.

MASC. I am completely in your power,

ERAS. Ha! Gros-Rene.

GR.-RE. Sir?

ERAS, I contradict a story, which I much fear is but too true. (To Mascarille). You wanted to run away.

MASC. Not in the least.

ERAS. What! Lucile is married to...

MASC. No, sir, I was only joking.

ERAS. Hey! you were joking, you wretch?

MASC. No, I was not joking.

ERAS. Is it true then?

MASC. No, I do not say that.

ERAS. What do you say then?

MASC. Alas! I say nothing, for fear of saying something wrong.

ERAS. Tell me positively, whether you have spoken the truth, or deceived me.

MASC. Whatever you please. I do not come here to contradict you.

ERAS. (***Drawing his sword***). Will you tell me? Here is something that will loosen your tongue without more ado.

MASC. It will again be saying some foolish speech or other. I pray you, if you have no objection, let me quickly have a few stripes, and then allow me to scamper off.

ERAS. You shall suffer death, unless you tell me the whole truth without disguise.

MASC. Alas! I will tell it then; but perhaps, sir, I shall make you angry.

ERAS. Speak: but take great care what you are doing; nothing shall save you from my just anger, if you utter but one single falsehood in your narration.

MASC. I agree to it; break my legs, arms, do worse to me still, kill me, if I have deceived you in the smallest degree, in anything I have said.

ERAS. It is true then that they are married?

MASC. With regard to this, I can now clearly see that my tongue tripped; but, for all that, the business happened just as I told you. It was after five visits paid at night, and whilst you were made use of as a screen to conceal their proceedings, that they were united the day before yesterday. Lucile ever since tries still more to hide the great love she bears my master, and desires he will only consider whatever he may see, and whatever favours she may show you, as the results of her deep-laid scheme, in order to prevent the discovery of their secrets. If, notwithstanding my protestations, you doubt the truth of what I have told you, Gros-Rene may come some night along with me, and I will show him, as I stand and watch, that we shall be admitted into her house, after dark.

ERAS. Out of my sight, villain.

MASC. I shall be delighted to go; that is just what I want. (*Exit*).

SCENE V.--ERASTE, GROS-RENE.

ERAS. Well?

GR.-RE. Well! Sir, we are both taken in if this fellow speaks the truth.

ERAS. Alas! The odious rascal has spoken the truth too well. All that he has said is very likely to have happened; Valere's behaviour, at the sight of this letter, denotes that there is a collusion between them, and that it is a screen to hide Lucile's love for him.

SCENE VI.--ERASTE, MARINETTE, GROS-RENE.

MAR. I come to tell you that this evening my mistress permits you to see her in the garden.

ERAS. How dare you address me, you hypocritical traitress? Get out of my sight, and tell your mistress not to trouble me any more with her letters; that is the regard, wretch, I have for them. (He tears the letter and goes out).

MAR. Tell me, Gros-Rene, what ails him?

GR.-RE. Dare you again address me, iniquitous female, deceitful crocodile, whose base heart is worse than a satrap or a Lestrigon?

[See Homer's Odyssey, X., v. 81-132.]

Go, go, carry your answer to your lovely mistress, and tell her short and sweet, that in spite of all her cunning, neither my master nor I are any longer fools, and that henceforth she and you may go to the devil together.   (***Exit***).

MAR. My poor Marinette, are you quite awake? What demon are they possessed by? What? Is it thus they receive our favours? How shocked my mistress will be when she hears this!

ACT II.

SCENE I.--ASCANIO, FROSINE.

FROS. Thank Heaven! I am a girl who can keep a secret, Ascanio.

ASC. But is this place private enough for such a conversation? Let us take care that nobody surprises us, or that we be not overheard from some corner or other.

FROS. We should be much less safe within the house; here we can easily see anybody coming, and may speak in perfect safety.

ASC. Alas! how painful it is for me to begin my tale!

FROS. Sure, this must be an important secret then?

ASC. Too much so, since I even entrust it to you with reluctance; even you should not know it, if I could keep it concealed any longer.

FROS. Fie! you insult me when you hesitate to trust in me, whom you have ever found so reserved in everything that concerns you--me, who was brought up with you, and have kept secret things of so great an importance to you; me, who know...

ASC. Yes, you are already acquainted with the secret reason which conceals from the eyes of the world my sex and family. You know that I was brought into this house, where I have passed my infancy, in order to preserve an inheritance which, on the death of young Ascanio (whom I personate), should have fallen to others; that is why I dare to unbosom myself to you with perfect confidence. But before we begin this conversation, Frosine, clear up a doubt which continually besets me. Can it be possible that Albert should know nothing of the secret, which thus disguises my sex, and makes him my father?

FROS. To tell you the truth, what you now wish to know has also greatly puzzled me. I have never been able to get at the bottom of this intrigue, nor could my mother give me any further insight. When Albert's son died, who was so much beloved, and to whom a very rich uncle bequeathed a great deal of property, even before his birth; his mother kept his death secret, fearing that her husband, who was absent at the time, would have gone distracted, had he seen that great inheritance, from which his family would have reaped such advantage, pass into the hands of another. She, I say, in order to conceal this misfortune formed the plan of putting you into the place of her lost son; you were taken from our family, where you were brought up. Your mother gave her consent to this deceit; you took the son's place, and every one was bribed to keep the secret. Albert has never known it through us, and as his wife kept it for more than twelve years, and died suddenly, her unexpected death prevented her from disclosing it. I perceive, however, that he keeps up an acquaintance with your real mother, and that, in private, he assists her; perhaps all this is not done without a reason. On the other hand, he commits a blunder by urging you to marry some young lady! Perhaps he knows that you took the place of his son, without knowing that you are a girl. But this digression might gradually carry us too far; let us return to that secret which I am impatient to hear.

ASC. Know then that Cupid cannot be deceived, that I have not been able to disguise my sex from love's eyes, and that his subtle shafts have reached the heart of a weak woman beneath the dress I wear. In four words, I am in love!

FROS. You in love!

ASC. Gently, Frosine; do not be quite so astonished; it is not time yet; this love-sick heart has something else to tell you that will surprise you.

FROS. What is it?

ASC. I am in love with Valere.

FROS. Ha! I really am surprised. What! you love a man whose family your deceit has deprived of a rich inheritance, and who, if he had the least suspicion of your sex, would immediately regain everything. This is a still greater subject of astonishment.

ASC. I have a more wonderful surprise for you yet in store--I am his wife.

FROS. Oh, Heavens! his wife!

ASC. Yes, his wife.

FROS. Ha! this is worse than all, and nearly drives me mad.

ASC. And yet this is not all.

FROS. Not all!

ASC. I am his wife, I say, and he does not think so, nor has he the least idea of what I really am.

FROS. Go on, I give it up, and will not say any thing more, so much every word amazes me. I cannot comprehend anything of these riddles.

ASC. I shall explain if you will but hear me. Valere who admired my sister, seemed to me a lover worthy of being listened to; I could not bear to see his addresses slighted without feeling a certain interest in him. I wished that Lucile should take pleasure in his conversation, I blamed her severity, and blamed it so effectually, that I myself, without being able to help it, became affected with that passion which she could not entertain. He was talking to her, and persuaded me; I suffered myself to be overcome by the very sighs he breathed; and the love, rejected by the object of his flame, entered, like a conqueror, into my heart, which was wounded by an arrow, not aimed at it, and paid another's debt with heavy interest. At last, my dear, the love I felt for him forced me to declare myself, but under a borrowed name. One night I spoke to him, disguising my voice as if it were Lucile's, and this too amiable lover thought she returned his love; I managed the conversation so well that he never found out the deception. Under that disguise which pleased so much his deluded imagination, I told him that I was enamoured of him, but that, finding my father opposed to my wishes, I ought at least to pretend to obey him; that therefore it behooved us to keep our love secret, with which the night alone should be acquainted; that all private conversation should be avoided during the day, for fear of betraying everything; that he should behold me with the same indifference as he did before we had come to an understanding; and that on his part, as well as mine, no communication should take place either by gesture, word, or writing. In short, without dwelling any longer upon all the pains I have taken to bring this deception to a safe termination, I went on with my bold project as far as it was possible to go, and secured the husband I mentioned to you.

FROS. Upon my word, you possess great talents. Would any one think so, on seeing her passionless countenance? However, you have been pretty hasty, and though I grant that the affair has succeeded until now, what do you think will be the end of it, for it cannot be long concealed?

ASC. When love is strong it overcomes all obstacles, until it is satisfied; provided it reaches the wished-for goal, it looks upon everything else as a mere trifle. I have told you all to-day, so that your advice... But here comes my husband.

SCENE II.--VALERE, ASCANIO, FROSINE.

VAL. If you are conversing, and if my presence is any interruption, I shall withdraw.

ASC. No; you may well interrupt it, since we were talking about you.

VAL. About me?

ASC. About yourself.

VAL. How so?

ASC. I was saying, that if I had been a woman, Valere would have been able to please me but too well, and that if I had been beloved by him, I should not have delayed long to make him happy.

VAL. This declaration does not cost you much, as there is such an *if* in the way; but you would be finely caught if some miraculous event should put to the proof the truth of so obliging a declaration.

ASC. Not in the least; I tell you that if I reigned in your heart, I would very willingly crown your passion.

VAL. And what, if you might contribute to my happiness, by assisting me to further my love?

ASC. I should then, certainly, disappoint you.

VAL. This admission is not very polite.

ASC. What, Valere? Supposing I were a woman and loved you tenderly, would you be so cruel as to make me promise to aid you in your love for another lady? I could not perform such a painful task.

VAL. But you are not a woman.

ASC. What I said to you I said in the character of a woman, and you ought to take it so.

VAL. Thus I ought not to imagine you like me, Ascanio, unless Heaven works a miracle in you. Therefore, as you are not a woman, I bid farewell to your affection; you do not care in the least for me.

ASC. My feelings are far more nice than people imagine, and the smallest misgiving shocks me when love is in the case. But I am sincere; I will not promise to aid you, Valere, unless you assure me that you entertain precisely the same sentiments for me; that you feel the same warmth of friendship for me as I feel for you; and that if I were a woman you would love no one better than me.

VAL. I never before heard of such a jealous scruple, but though quite unexpected, this affection obliges me to make some return for it; I here promise you all you require of me.

ASC. But sincerely?

VAL. Yes, sincerely.

ASC. If this be true, I promise you that henceforth your interests shall be mine.

VAL. I have a secret of the utmost consequence to reveal to you by and by, and then I shall remind you of your words.

ASC. And I have likewise a secret to discover to you, wherein your affection for me may show itself.

VAL. Indeed! what can that be?

ASC. I have a love affair which I dare not reveal, and you have influence enough over the object of my passion to promote my happiness.

VAL. Explain yourself, Ascanio, and be assured beforehand that, if your happiness lies in my power, it is certain.

ASC. You promise more than you imagine.

VAL. No, no; tell me the name of the person whom I have to influence.

ASC. It is not yet time, but it is a person who is nearly related to you.

VAL. Your words amaze me; would to Heaven my sister...

ASC. This is not the proper time to explain myself, I tell you.

VAL. Why so?

ASC. For a certain reason. You shall know my secret when I know yours.

VAL. I must have another person's permission before I can discover it to you.

ASC. Obtain it then; and when we shall have explained ourselves we shall see which of us two will best keep his word.

VAL. Farewell, I accept your offer.

ASC. And I will be bound by it, Valere. (***Exit Valere***.)

FROS. He thinks you will help him as a brother.

SCENE III.--LUCILE, ASCANIO, MARINETTE, FROSINE.

LUC. (***Saying the first words to Marinette***). I have done it; it is thus I can revenge myself; if this step torments him, it will be a great consolation to me... Brother, you perceive a change in me; I am resolved to love Valere, after so much ill-usage; he shall become the object of my affection.

ASC. What do you say, sister? How do you change so suddenly? This inconstancy seems to me very strange.

LUC. Your change of disposition has more cause to surprise me. You
formerly used always to plead in favour of Valere; for his sake you have
accused me of caprice, blind cruelty, pride and injustice; and now, when
I wish to love him, my intention displeases you, and I find you speaking
against his interest.

ASC. I abandon his interest, sister, out of regard to yours. I know he
is under the sway of another fair one; it will be a discredit to your
charms if you call him back, and he does not come.

LUC. If that is all, I shall take care not to suffer a defeat; I know
what I am to believe of his passion; he has shown it very clearly, at
least so I think; you may safely discover my sentiments to him: or if
you refuse to do it, I, myself shall let him know that his passion has
touched me. What! you stand thunderstruck, brother, at those words!

ASC. Oh, sister, if I have any influence over you, if you will listen to
a brother's entreaties, abandon such a design; do not take away Valere
from the love of a young creature, in whom I feel great interest, and
for whom, upon my word, you ought to feel some sympathy. The poor
unfortunate woman loves him to distraction; to me alone she has
disclosed her passion; I perceive in her heart such a tender affection,
that it might soften even the most relentless being. Yes, you yourself
will pity her condition when she shall become aware with what stroke you
threaten to crush her love; so sure am I of the excess of her grief,
that I am certain, sister, she will die, if you rob her of the man she
adores. Eraste is a match that ought to satisfy you, and the mutual
affection you have for one another...

LUC. Brother, it is sufficient! I do not know in whom you take such an
interest; but let us not continue this conversation, I beg of you; leave

me a little to my own thoughts.

ASC. Cruel sister, you will drive me to despair if you carry your design into execution.

SCENE IV.--LUCILE, MARINETTE.

MAR. Your resolution, madam, is very sudden.

LUC. A heart considers nothing when it is once affronted, but flies to its revenge, and eagerly lays hold of whatever it thinks can minister to its resentment. The wretch! To treat me with such extreme insolence!

MAR. You see I have not yet recovered the effects; though I were to brood over it to all eternity, I cannot understand it, and all my labour is in vain. For never did a lover express more delight on receiving good news; so pleased was he with your kind note that he called me nothing less than a divine creature; and yet, when I brought him the other message, there was never a poor girl treated so scurvily. I cannot imagine what could happen in so short a time to occasion so great a change.

LUC. Do not trouble yourself about what may have happened, since nothing shall secure him against my hatred. What! do you think there is any secret reason for this affront but his own baseness? Does the unfortunate letter I sent him, and for which I now blame myself, present the smallest excuse for his madness?

MAR. Indeed, I must say you are right; this quarrel is downright treachery; we have both been duped, and yet, madam, we listen to these faithless rascals who promise everything; who, in order to hook us, feign so much tenderness; we let our severity melt before their fine speeches, and yield to their wishes, because we are too weak! A shame on our folly, and a plague take the men!

LUC. Well, well! let him boast and laugh at us; he shall not long have cause to triumph; I will let him see that in a well-balanced mind hatred follows close on slighted favours.

MAR. At least, in such a case, it is a great happiness to know that we are not in their power. Notwithstanding all that was said, Marinette was right the other night to interfere when some people were in a very merry mood. Another, in hopes of matrimony, would have listened to the temptation, but *nescio vos*, quoth I.

[These two Latin words, which were in very common use in France, during Moliere's time, are taken from the Vulgate, Matthew xxv. 12: "Domine, domine, aperi nobis."--At ille respondens ait: "Amen dico vobis, nescio vos."]

LUC. How foolishly you talk; how ill you choose your time to joke! My heart is full of grief. If ever fate wills it that this false lover,--but I am in the wrong to conceive at present any such expectation; for Heaven has been too well pleased to afflict me to put it in my power to be revenged on him,--but if ever a propitious fate, I say, should cause Eraste to come back to me, and lay down his life as a sacrifice at my feet, as well as declare his sorrow for what he has done to-day, I forbid you, above all things, to speak to me in his favour. On the contrary, I would have you show your zeal by setting fully before me the greatness of his crime; if my heart should be tempted ever to degrade itself so far, let your affection then show itself; spare me not, but support my anger as is fit.

MAR. Oh! do not fear! leave that to me; I am at least as angry as you; I would rather remain a maid all my life than that my fa- rascal should give me any inclination for him again. If he comes...

SCENE V.--MARINETTE, LUCILE, ALBERT.

ALB. Go in, Lucile, and tell the tutor to come to me; I wish to have a little talk with him; and as he is the master of Ascanio, find out what is the cause that the latter has been of late so gloomy.

SCENE VI.--ALBERT, *alone*.

Into what an abyss of cares and perplexities does one unjust action precipitate us. For a long time I have suffered a great deal because I was too avaricious, and passed off a stranger for my dead son. When I consider the mischief which followed I sincerely wish I had never thought of it. Sometimes I dread to behold my family in poverty and covered with shame, when the deception will be found out; at other times I fear a hundred accidents that may happen to this son whom it concerns me so much to preserve. If any business calls me abroad, I am afraid of hearing, on my return, some such melancholy tidings as these: "You know, I suppose? Have they not told you? Your son has a fever; or he has broken his leg or his arm." In short, every moment, no matter what I do, all kinds of apprehensions are continually entering into my head. Ha!

SCENE VII.--ALBERT, METAPHRASTUS.

MET. *Mandatum tuum euro diligenter*.

["I hasten to obey your order."]

ALB. Master, I want to...

MET. Master is derived from *magis ter*; it is as though you say "thrice greater."

ALB. May I die if I knew that; but, never mind, be it so. Master, then...

MET. Proceed.

ALB. So I would, but do not proceed to interrupt me thus. Once more, then, master, for the third time, my son causes me some uneasiness. You know that I love him, and that I always brought him up carefully.

MET. It is true: *filio non potest praeferri nisi filius*.

["To a son one can only prefer a son." An allusion to an article of feudal law.]

ALB. Master, I do not think this jargon at all necessary in common conversation. I believe you are a great Latin scholar and an eminent doctor, for I rely on those who have told me so; but in a conversation which I should like to have with you, do not display all your learning--do not play the pedant, and utter ever so many words, as if you were holding forth in a pulpit. My father, though he was a very clever man, never taught me anything but my prayers; and though I have said them daily for fifty years, they are still High-Dutch to me. Therefore, do not employ your prodigious knowledge, but adapt your language to my weak understanding.

MET. Be it so.

ALB. My son seems to be afraid of matrimony; whenever I propose a match to him, he seems indifferent, and draws back.

MET. Perhaps he is of the temper of Mark Tully's brother, whom he writes about to Atticus. This is what the Greeks call *athanaton* ....

[Immortal.]

ALB. For Heaven's sake! you ceaseless teacher, I pray you have done with the Greeks, the Albanians, the Sclavonians, and all the other nations you have mentioned; they have nothing to do with my son.

MET. Well then, your son...?

ALB. I do not know whether a secret love does not burn within him. Something disturbs him, or I am much deceived; for I saw him yesterday, when he did not see me, in a corner of the wood, where no person ever goes.

MET. In a recess of a grove, you mean, a remote spot, in Latin *secessus*. Virgil says, *est in secessu locus* ...

["There is a remote spot"]

ALB. How could Virgil say that, since I am certain that there was not a soul in that quiet spot except us two?

MET. I quote Virgil as a famous author, who employed a more correct expression than the word you used, and not as a witness of what you saw yesterday.

ALB. I tell you I do not need a more correct expression, an author, or a witness, and that my own testimony is sufficient.

MET. However, you ought to choose words which are used by the best authors: *tu vivendo bonos, scribendo sequare peritos*, as the saying is.

["Regulate your conduct after the example of good people, your style after good authors."]

ALB. Man or devil, will you hear me without disputing?

MET. That is Quintilian's rule.

ALB. Hang the chatterbox!

MET. He has a very learned sentence upon a similar subject, which, I am sure, you will be very glad to hear.

ALB. I will be the devil to carry you off, you wretch. Oh! I am very much tempted to apply something to those chops.

MET. Sir, what is the reason that you fly in such a passion! What do you wish me to do?

ALB. I have told you twenty times; I wish you to listen to me when I speak.

MET. Oh! undoubtedly, you shall be satisfied if that is all. I am silent.

ALB. You act wisely.

MET. I am ready to hear what you have to say.

ALB. So much the better.

MET. May I be struck dead if I say another word!

ALB. Heaven grant you that favour.

MET. You shall not accuse me henceforth of talkativeness.

ALB. Be it so.

MET. Speak whenever you please.

ALB. I am going to do so.

MET. And do not be afraid of my interrupting you.

ALB. That is enough.

MET. My word is my bond.

ALB. I believe so.

MET. I have promised to say nothing.

ALB. That is sufficient.

MET. From this moment I am dumb.

ALB. Very well.

MET. Speak; go on; I will give you a hearing at least; you shall not complain that I cannot keep silent; I will not so much as open my mouth.

ALB. (*Aside*). The wretch!

MET. But pray, do not be prolix. I have listened already a long time, and it is reasonable that I should speak in my turn.

ALB. Detestable torturer!

MET. Hey! good lack! would you have me listen to you for ever? Let us share the talk, at least, or I shall be gone.

ALB. My patience is really...

MET. What, will you proceed? You have not done yet? By Jove, I am stunned.

ALB. I have not spoken...

MET. Again! good Heavens! what exuberant speechifying! Can nothing be done to stop it?

ALB. I am mad with rage.

MET. You are talking again! What a peculiar way of tormenting people! Let me say a few words, I entreat you; a fool who says nothing cannot be distinguished from a wise man who holds his tongue.

ALB. Zounds! I will make you hold yours. (***Exit***).

SCENE VIII.--METAPHRASTUS, *alone*.

Hence comes very properly that saying of a philosopher, "Speak, that I may know thee." Therefore, if the liberty of speaking is taken from me, I, for my part, would as soon be divested of my humanity, and exchange my being for that of a brute. I shall have a headache for a week. Oh! how I detest these eternal talkers! But if learned men are not listened to, if their mouths are for ever to be stopped, then the order of events must be changed; the hens in a little time will devour the fox; young children teach old men; little lambs take a delight in pursuing the wolf; fools make laws; women go to battle; judges be tried by criminals; and masters whipped by pupils; a sick man prescribe for a healthy one; a timorous hare...

SCENE IX.--ALBERT, METAPHRASTUS.

(Albert rings a bell in the ears of Metaphrastus, and drives him off).

MET. Mercy on me! Help! help!

ACT III.

SCENE I.--MASCARILLE, *alone*.

Heaven sometimes favours a bold design; we must get out of a bad business as well as we can. As for me, after having imprudently talked too much, the quickest remedy I could employ was to go on in the same way, and immediately to tell to our old master the whole intrigue. His son is a giddy-brained mortal, who worries me; but if the other tells what I have discovered to him, then I had better take care, for I shall get a beating. However, before his fury can be kindled, some lucky thing may happen to us, and the two old men may arrange the business between themselves. That is what I am going to attempt; without losing a moment I must, by my master's order, go and see Albert. (Knocks at Albert's door).

SCENE II.--ALBERT, MASCARILLE.

ALB. Who knocks?

MASC. A friend.

ALB. What brings you hither, Mascarille?

MASC. I come, sir, to wish you good-morning.

ALB. Hah! you really take a great deal of pains. Good-morning, then, with all my heart. (*He goes in*).

MASC. The answer is short and sweet. What a blunt old fellow he is. (*Knocks*).

ALB. What, do you knock again?

MASC. You have not heard me, sir.

ALB. Did you not wish me good-morning?

MASC. I did.

ALB. Well, then, good morning I say. (*Is going; Mascarille stops him*).

MASC. But I likewise come to pay Mr. Polydore's compliments to you.

ALB. Oh! that is another thing. Has your master ordered you to give his compliments to me?

MASC. Yes.

ALB. I am obliged to him; you may go; tell him I wish him all kind of happiness. (*Exit*).

MASC. This man is an enemy to all ceremony. (*Knocks*). I have not finished, sir, giving you his whole message; he has a favour to request of you.

ALB. Well, whenever he pleases, I am at his service.

MASC. (*Stopping him*). Stay, and allow me to finish in two words. He desires to have a few minutes' conversation with you about an important affair, and he will come hither.

ALB. Hey! what affair can that be which makes him wish to have some conversation with me?

MASC. A great secret, I tell you, which he has but just discovered, and which, no doubt, greatly concerns you both. And now I have delivered my message.

SCENE III.--ALBERT, *alone*.

ALB. Righteous Heavens! how I tremble! Polydore and I have had little acquaintance together; my designs will all be overthrown; this secret is, no doubt, that of which I dread the discovery. They have bribed somebody to betray me; so there is a stain upon my honour which can never be wiped off. My imposture is found out. Oh! how difficult it is to keep the truth concealed for any length of time! How much better would it have been for me and my reputation had I followed the dictates of a well-founded apprehension! Many times and oft have I been tempted to give up to Polydore the wealth I withhold from him, in order to prevent the outcry that will be raised against me when everything shall be known, and so get the whole business quietly settled. But, alas! it is now too late, the opportunity is gone, and this wealth, which wrongfully came into my family, will be lost to them, and sweep away the greatest part of my own property with it.

SCENE IV.--ALBERT, POLYDORE.

POL. (*Not seeing Albert*). To be married in this fashion, and no one knowing anything about it! I hope it may all end well! I do not know what to think of it; I much fear the great wealth and just anger of the father. But I see him alone.

ALB. Oh, Heavens! yonder comes Polydore.

POL. I tremble to accost him.

ALB. Fear keeps me back.

POL. How shall I begin?

ALB. What shall I say?

POL. He is in a great passion.

ALB. He changes colour.

POL. I see, Signor Albert, by your looks, that you know already what brings me hither.

ALB. Alas! yes.

POL. The news, indeed, may well surprise you, and I could scarcely believe what I was told just now.

ALB. I ought to blush with shame and confusion.

POL. I think such an action deserves great blame, and do not pretend to excuse the guilty.

ALB. Heaven is merciful to miserable sinners.

POL. You should bear this in mind.

ALB. A man ought to behave as a Christian.

POL. That is quite right.

ALB. Have mercy; for Heaven's sake, have mercy, Signor Polydore.

POL. It is for me to implore it of you.

ALB. Grant me mercy; I ask it on my bended knees.

POL. I ought to be in that attitude rather than you.

[The two old men are kneeling opposite to one another.]

ALB. Pity my misfortune.

POL. After such an outrage I am the postulant.

ALB. Your goodness is heart-rending.

POL. You abash me with so much humility.

ALB. Once more, pardon.

POL. Alas! I crave it of you.

ALB. I am extremely sorry for this business.

POL. And I feel it greatly.

ALB. I venture to entreat you not to make it public.

POL. Alas, Signor Albert, I desire the very same.

ALB. Let us preserve my honour.

POL. With all my heart.

ALB. As for money, you shall determine how much you require.

POL. I desire no more than you are willing to give; you shall be the master in all these things, I shall be but too happy if you are so.

ALB. Ha! what a God-like man! how very kind he is!

POL. How very kind you are yourself, and that after such a misfortune.

ALB. May you be prosperous in all things!

POL. May Heaven preserve you!

ALB. Let us embrace like brothers.

POL. With all my heart! I am overjoyed that everything has ended so happily,

ALB. I thank Heaven for it.

POL. I do not wish to deceive you; I was afraid you would resent that Lucile has committed a fault with my son; and as you are powerful, have wealth and friends...

ALB. Hey! what do you say of faults and Lucile?

POL. Enough, let us not enter into a useless conversation. I own my son is greatly to blame; nay, if that will satisfy you, I will admit that he alone is at fault; that your daughter was too virtuous, and would never have taken a step so derogatory to honour, had she not been prevailed upon by a wicked seducer; that the wretch has betrayed her innocent modesty, and thus frustrated all your expectations. But since the thing is done, and my prayers have been granted, since we are both at peace and amity, let it be buried in oblivion, and repair the offence by the ceremony of a happy alliance.

ALB. (*Aside*). Oh, Heavens! what a mistake I have been under! What do I hear? I get from one difficulty into another as great. I do not know what to answer amidst these different emotions; if I say one word, I am afraid of betraying myself.

POL. What are you thinking of, Signor Albert?

ALB. Of nothing. Let us put off our conversation for a while, I pray you. I have become suddenly very unwell, and am obliged to leave you.

SCENE V.--POLYDORE, *alone*.

I can look into his soul and discover what disturbs him; though he listened to reason at first, yet his anger is not quite appeased. Now and then the remembrance of the offence flashes upon him; he endeavours to hide his emotion by leaving me alone. I feel for him, and his grief touches me. It will require some time before he regains his composure, for if sorrow is suppressed too much, it easily becomes worse. O! here comes my foolish boy, the cause of all this confusion.

SCENE VI.--POLYDORE, VALERE.

POL. So, my fine fellow, shall your nice goings-on disturb your poor old father every moment? You perform something new every day, and we never hear of anything else.

VAL. What am I doing every day that is so very criminal? And how have I deserved so greatly a father's wrath?

POL. I am a strange man, and very peculiar to accuse so good and discreet a son. He lives like a saint, and is at prayers and in the house from morning to evening. It is a great untruth to say that he perverts the order of nature, and turns day into night! It is a horrible falsehood to state that upon several occasions he has shown no consideration for father or kindred; that very lately he married secretly the daughter of Albert, regardless of the great consequences that were sure to follow; they mistake him for some other! The poor innocent creature does not even know what I mean! Oh, you villain! whom Heaven has sent me as a punishment for my sins, will you always do as you like, and shall I never see you act discreetly as long as I live? (*Exit*).

VAL. (*Alone, musing*). Whence comes this blow? I am perplexed, and can find none to think of but Mascarille, he will never confess it to me; I must be cunning, and curb my well-founded anger a little.

SCENE VII.--VALERE, MASCARILLE.

VAL. Mascarille, my father whom I just saw knows our whole secret.

MASC. Does he know it?

VAL. Yes.

MASC. How the deuce could he know it?

VAL. I do not know whom to suspect; but the result has been so successful, that I have all the reason in the world to be delighted. He has not said one cross word about it; he excuses my fault, and approves of my love; I would fain know who could have made him so tractable. I cannot express to you the satisfaction it gives me.

MASC. And what would you say, sir, if it was I who had procured you this piece of good luck?

VAL. Indeed! you want to deceive me.

MASC. It is I, I tell you, who told it to your father, and produced this happy result for you.

VAL. Really, without jesting?

MASC. The devil take me if I jest, and if it is not as I tell you.

VAL. (***Drawing his sword***). And may he take me if I do not this very moment reward you for it.

MASC. Ha, sir! what now? Don't surprise me.

VAL. Is this the fidelity you promised me? If I had not deceived you, you would never have owned the trick which I rightly suspected you played me. You rascal! your tongue, too ready to wag, has provoked my father's wrath against me, and utterly ruined me. You shall die without saying another word.

MASC. Gently; my soul is not in a fit condition to die. I entreat you, be kind enough to await the result of this affair. I had very good reasons for revealing a marriage which you yourself could hardly conceal. It was a masterpiece of policy; you will not find your rage justified by the issue. Why should you get angry if, through me, you get all you desire, and are freed from the constraint you at present lie under?

VAL. And what if all this talk is nothing but moonshine?

MASC. Why, then, it will be time enough to kill me; but my schemes may perchance succeed. Heaven will assist his own servants; you will be satisfied in the end, and thank me for my extraordinary management.

VAL. Well, we shall see. But Lucile...

MASC. Hold, here comes her father

SCENE VIII.--ALBERT, VALERE, MASCARILLE.

ALB. (*Not seeing Valere*). The more I recover from the confusion into which I fell at first, the more I am astonished at the strange things Polydore told me, and which my fear made me interpret in so different a manner to what he intended. Lucile maintains that it is all nonsense, and spoke to me in such a manner as leaves no room for suspicion... Ha! sir, it is you whose unheard-of impudence sports with my honour, and invents this base story?

MASC. Pray, Signor Albert, use milder terms, and do not be so angry with your son-in-law.

ALB. How! son-in-law, rascal? You look as if you were the main-spring of this intrigue, and the originator of it.

MASC. Really I see no reason for you to fly in such a passion.

ALB. Pray, do you think it right to take away the character of my daughter, and bring such a scandal upon a whole family?

MASC. He is ready to do all you wish.

ALB. I only want him to tell the truth. If he had any inclination for Lucile, he should have courted her in an honourable and open way; he should have acted as he ought, and asked her father's leave; and not have had recourse to this cowardly contrivance, which offends modesty so much.

MASC. What! Lucile is not secretly engaged to my master?

ALB. No, rascal, nor ever will be.

MASC. Not quite so fast! If the thing is already done, will you give your consent to ratify that secret engagement?

ALB. And if it is certain that it is not so, will you have your bones broken?

VAL. It is easy, sir, to prove to you that he speaks the truth.

ALB. Good! there is the other! Like master, like man. O! what impudent liars!

MASC. Upon the word of a man of honour, it is as I say.

VAL. Why should we deceive you?

ALB. (*Aside*) They are two sharpers that know how to play into each other's hands.

MASC. But let us come to the proof, and without quarrelling. Send for

Lucile, and let her speak for herself.

ALB. And what if she should prove you a liar?

MASC. She will not contradict us, sir; of that I am certain. Promise to give your consent to their engagement; and I will suffer the severest punishment if, with her own mouth, she does not confess to you that she is engaged to Valere, and shares his passion.

ALB. We shall see this presently. (***He knocks at his door***).

MASC. (To Valere). Courage, Sir; all will end well.

ALB. Ho! Lucile, one word with you.

VAL. (***To Mascarille***), I fear...

MASC. Fear nothing.

SCENE IX.--VALERE, ALBERT, LUCILE, MASCAR-ILLE.

MASC. Signor Albert, at least be silent. At length, madam, everything conspires to make your happiness complete. Your father, who is informed of your love, leaves you your husband and gives his permission to your union, provided that, banishing all frivolous fears, a few words from your own mouth corroborate what we have told him.

LUC. What nonsense does this impudent scoundrel tell me?

MASC. That is all right. I am already honoured with a fine title.

LUC. Pray, sir, who has invented this nice story which has been spread about today?

VAL. Pardon me, charming creature. My servant has been babbling; our marriage is discovered, without my consent.

LUC. Our marriage?

VAL. Everything is known, adorable Lucile; it is vain to dissemble.

LUC. What! the ardour of my passion has made you my husband?

VAL. It is a happiness which causes a great many heart-burnings. But I impute the successful result of my courtship less to your great passion for me than to your kindness of heart. I know you have cause to be offended, that it was the secret which you would fain have concealed. I myself have put a restraint on my ardour, so that I might not violate your express commands; but...

MASC. Yes, it was I who told it. What great harm is done?

LUC. Was there ever a falsehood like this? Dare you mention this in my very presence, and hope to obtain my hand by this fine contrivance? What a wretched lover you are--you, whose gallant passion would wound my honour, because it could not gain my heart; who wish to frighten my father by a foolish story, so that you might obtain my hand as a reward for having vilified me. Though everything were favourable to your love--my father, fate, and my own inclination--yet my well-founded resentment would struggle against my own inclination, fate, and my father, and even lose life rather than be united to one who thought to obtain my hand in this manner. Begone! If my sex could with decency be provoked to any outburst of rage, I would let you know what it was to treat me thus.

VAL. (*To Mascarille*). It is all over with us; her anger cannot be appeased.

MASC. Let me speak to her. Prithee, madam, what is the good of all these excuses? What are you thinking of? And what strange whim makes you thus oppose your own happiness? If your father were a harsh parent, the case would be different, but he listens to reason; and he himself has assured me that if you would but confess the truth, his affection would grant you everything. I believe you are a little ashamed frankly to acknowledge that you have yielded to love; but if you have lost a trifling amount of freedom, everything will be set to rights again by a good marriage. Your great love for Valere may be blamed a little, but the mischief is not so great as if you had murdered a man. We all know that flesh is frail, and that a maid is neither stock nor stone. You were not the first, that is certain; and you will not be the last, I dare say.

LUC. What! can you listen to this shameless talk, and make no reply to these indignities?

ALB. What would you have me say? This affair puts me quite beside myself.

MASC. Upon my word, madam, you ought to have confessed all before now.

LUC. What ought I to have confessed?

MASC. What? Why, what has passed between my master and you. A fine

joke,
indeed!

LUC. Why, what has passed between your master and me, impudent wretch?

MASC. You ought, I think, to know that better than I; you passed that night too agreeably, to make us believe you could forget it so soon.

LUC. Father, we have too long borne with the insolence of an impudent lackey. (***Gives him a box on the ear***).

SCENE X.--ALBERT, VALERE, MASCARILLE.

MASC. I think she gave me a box on the ear.

ALB. Be gone! rascal, villain! Her father approves the way in which she has made her hand felt upon your cheek.

MASC. May be so; yet may the devil take me if I said anything but what was true!

ALB. And may I lose an ear if you carry on this impudence any further!

MASC. Shall I send for two witnesses to testify to the truth of my statements?

ALB. Shall I send for two of my servants to give you a sound thrashing?

MASC. Their testimony will corroborate mine.

ALB. Their arms may make up for my want of strength.

MASC. I tell you, Lucile behaves thus because she is ashamed.

ALB. I tell you, you shall be answerable for all this.

MASC. Do you know Ormin, that stout and clever notary?

ALB. Do you know Grimpant, the city executioner?

MASC. And Simon, the tailor, who used formerly to work for all the people of fashion?

ALB. And the gibbet set up in the middle of the market-place?

MASC. You shall see they will confirm the truth of this marriage.

ALB. You shall see they will make an end of you.

MASC. They were the witnesses chosen by them.

ALB. They shall shortly revenge me on you.

MASC. I myself saw them at the altar.

ALB. And I myself shall see you with a halter.

MASC. By the same token, your daughter had a black veil on.

ALB. By the same token, your face foretells your doom.

MASC. What an obstinate old man.

ALB. What a cursed rascal! You may thank my advanced years, which prevent me from punishing your insulting remarks upon the spot: but I promise you, you shall be paid with full interest.

SCENE XI.--VALERE, MASCARILLE.

VAL. Well, where is now that fine result you were to produce...?

MASC. I understand what you mean. Everything goes against me: I see cudgels and gibbets preparing for me on every side. Therefore, so that I may be at rest amidst this chaos, I shall go and throw myself headlong from a rock, if, in my present despair, I can find one high enough to please me. Farewell, sir.

VAL. No, no; in vain you wish to fly. If you die, I expect it to be in my presence.

MASC. I cannot die if anybody is looking on: it would only delay my end.

VAL. Follow me traitor; follow me. My maddened love will soon show whether this is a jesting matter or not.

MASC. (*Alone*). Unhappy Mascarille, to what misfortunes are you condemned to-day for another's sin!

*　　*　　*　　*　　*

ACT IV.

SCENE I.--ASCANIO, FROSINE.

FROS. What has happened is very annoying.

ASC. My dear Frosine, fate has irrevocably decreed my ruin. Now the affair has gone so far, it will never stop there, but will go on; Lucile and Valere, surprised at such a strange mystery, will, one day, try to find their way amidst this darkness, and thus all my plans will miscarry. For, whether Albert is acquainted with the deception, or whether he himself is deceived, as well as the rest of the world, if ever it happens that my family is discovered, and all the wealth he has wrongfully acquired passes into the hands of others, judge if he will then endure my presence; for, not having any interest more in the matter, he will abandon me, and his affection for me will be at an end. Whatever, then, my lover may think of my deception, will he acknowledge as his wife a girl without either fortune or family?

FROS. I think you reason rightly; but these reflections should have come sooner. What has prevented you from seeing all this before? there was no need to be a witch to foresee, as soon as you fell in love with Valere, all that your genius never found out until to-day. It is the natural consequence of what you have done; as soon as I was made acquainted with it I never imagined it would end otherwise.

ASC. But what must I do? There never was such a misfortune as mine. Put yourself in my place, and give me advice.

FROS. If I put myself in your place, you will have to give me advice upon this ill-success; for I am you, and you are I. Counsel me, Frosine, in the condition I am in. Where can we find a remedy? Tell me, I beg of you.

ASC. Alas! do not make fun of me. You show but little sympathy with my bitter grief, if you laugh in the midst of my distress.

FROS. Really, Ascanio, I pity your distress, and would do my utmost to help you. But what can I do, after all? I see very little likelihood of arranging this affair so as to satisfy your love.

ASC. If no assistance can be had, I must die.

FROS. Die! Come, come; it is always time enough for that. Death is a remedy ever at hand; we ought to make use of it as late as possible.

ASC. No, no, Frosine. If you and your invaluable counsels do not guide me amidst all these breakers, I abandon myself wholly to despair.

FROS. Do you know what I am thinking about? I must go and see the.... But here comes Eraste; he may interrupt us. We will talk this matter over as we go along. Come, let us retire.

[Frosine means by "the..." the woman who knows the secret of all this intrigue, and who is supposed to be the mother of Ascanio. This is explained later on in Act V., Scene 4]

SCENE II.--ERASTE, GROS-RENE.

ERAS. You have failed again?

GR.-RE. Never was an ambassador less listened to. No sooner had I told
her that you desired to have a moment's conversation with her, than,
drawing herself up, she answered haughtily, "Go, go, I value your master
just as much as I do you; tell him he may go about his business;" and
after this fine speech she turned her head away from me and walked off.
Marinette, too, imitating her mistress, said, with a disdainful sneer,
"Begone, you low fellow," and then left me; so that your fortune and mine
are very much alike.

[In the original it is **beau valet de carreau**. Littre,
in his "Dictionaire de la langue francaise," says that this word which
means literally "knave of diamonds," was considered an insult, because in
the old packs of cards of the beginning of the seventeenth century, that
knave was called **valet de chasse**, hunting servant, a rather
menial situation; while the knave of spades, **valet de pique**, was
called, nobleman's servant; the knave of hearts, valet de coeur, valet
de cour, court servant; and the knave of clubs, valet de trefle,
valet de pied, foot servant.]

ERAS. What an ungrateful creature, to receive with so much haughtiness
the quick return of a heart justly incensed. Is the first outburst of a
passion, which with so much reason thought itself deceived, unworthy of
excuse? Could I, when burning with love, remain insensible, in that
fatal moment, to the happiness of a rival? Would any other not have
acted in the same way as I did, or been less amazed at so much boldness?
Was I not quick in abandoning my well-founded suspicions? I did not wait

till she swore they were false. When no one can tell as yet what to think of it, my heart, full of impatience, restores Lucile to her former place, and seeks to find excuses for her. Will not all these proofs satisfy her of the ardour of my respectful passion? Instead of calming my mind, and providing me with arms against a rival who wishes to alarm me, this ungrateful woman abandons me to all the tortures of jealousy, and refuses to receive my messages and notes, or to grant me an interview. Alas! that love is certainly very lukewarm which can be extinguished by so trifling an offence; that scornful rigour, which is displayed so readily, sufficiently shows to me the depth of her affection. What value ought I to set now upon all the caprices with which she fanned my love? No! I do not pretend to be any longer the slave of one who has so little love for me; since she does not mind whether she keeps me or not, I will do the same.

GR.-RE. And so will I. Let us both be angry, and put our love on the list of our old sins; we must teach a lesson to that wayward sex, and make them feel that we possess some courage. He that will bear their contempt shall have enough of it. If we had sense enough not to make ourselves too cheap, women would not talk so big. Oh! how insolent they are through our weakness! May I be hanged if we should not see them fall upon our neck more often than we wished, if it was not for those servilities with which most men, now-a-days, continually spoil them.

ERAS. As for me, nothing vexes me so much as contempt; and to punish her's by one as great, I am resolved to cherish a new passion.

GR.-RE. So will I, and never trouble my head about women again. I renounce them all, and believe honestly you could not do better than to act like me. For, master, people say that woman is an animal hard to be known, and naturally very prone to evil; and as an animal is always an animal, and will never be anything but an animal, though it lived for a hundred thousand years, so, without contradiction, a woman is always a woman, and will never be anything but a woman as long as the world endures.

[This passage is paraphrased from Erasmus, Colloquia familiaria et Encomium Moriae, in which, after having called a woman ***animal stultum atque ineptum verum ridiculum, et suave***, Folly adds, Quemadmodum, juxta Graecorum proverbium, simia semper est simia, etiamsi purpura vestiatur, ita mulier semper mulier est, hoc est stulta, quamcunque personam induxerit.]

Wherefore, as a certain Greek author says: a woman's head is like a quicksand; for pray, mark well this argument, which is most weighty: As the head is the chief of the body, and as the body without a chief is worse than a beast, unless the chief has a good understanding with the body, and unless everything be as well regulated as if it were measured with a pair of compasses, we see certain confusions arrive; the animal part then endeavours to get the better of the rational, and, we see one pull to the right, another to the left; one wants something soft, another something hard; in short, everything goes topsy turvy. This is to show that here below, as it has been explained to me, a woman's head is like a weather-cock on the top of a house, which veers about at the slightest breeze; that is why cousin Aristotle often compares her to the sea; hence people say that nothing in the world is so stable as the waves.

[Though "stable" is here used, it is only employed to show the confusion of Gros-Rene's ideas, who, of course, wishes to say "unstable."]

Now, by comparison--for comparison makes us comprehend an argument distinctly,--and we learned men love a comparison better than a similitude,--by comparison, then, if you please, master, as we see that the sea, when a storm rises, begins to rage, the wind roars and destroys, billows dash against billows with a great hullabaloo, and the ship, in spite of the mariner, goes sometimes down to the cellar and sometimes up into the garret; so, when a woman gets whims and crotchets into her head, we see a tempest in the form of a violent storm, which will break out by certain ... words, and then a ... certain wind, which by ... certain waves in ... a certain manner, like a sand-bank ... when ... In short, woman is worse than the devil.

[This long speech of Gros-Rene ridicules the pedantic arguments of some of the philosophers of the time of Moliere. It also attributes to the ancients some sayings of authors of the day; for example, the comparison, from a Greek author, "that a woman's head is like a quicksand," is from a contemporary; the saying from Aristotle, comparing woman to the sea, is from Malherbe. Words very familiar look more homely when employed with high-flown language, and Gros-Rene's speech is no bad example of this, whilst at the same time it becomes more muddled the longer it goes on. There exists also a tradition that the actor who performs the part of Gros-Rene should in order to show his confusion, when he says "goes sometimes down the cellar," point to his head, and when he mentions "up into the garret," point to his feet.]

ERAS. You have argued that very well.

GR.-RE. Pretty well, thanks to Heaven; but I see them coming this way, sir,--stand firm.

ERAS. Never fear.

GR.-RE. I am very much afraid that her eyes will ensnare you again.

SCENE III.--ERASTE, LUCILE, MARINETTE, GROS-RENE.

MAR. He is not gone yet, but do not yield.

LUC. Do not imagine I am so weak.

MAR. He comes towards us.

ERAS. No, no, madam, do not think that I have come to speak to you again of my passion; it is all over; I am resolved to cure myself. I know how little share I have in your heart. A resentment kept up so long for a slight offence shows me your indifference but too plainly, and I must tell you that contempt, above all things, wounds a lofty mind. I confess I saw in you charms which I never found in any other; the delight I took in my chains would have made me prefer them to sceptres, had they been offered to me. Yes, my love for you was certainly very great; my life was centred in you; I will even own that, though I am insulted, I shall still perhaps have difficulty enough to free myself. Maybe, notwithstanding the cure I am attempting, my heart may for a long time smart with this wound. Freed from a yoke which I was happy to bend under, I shall take a resolution never to love again. But no matter, since your hatred repulses a heart which love brings back to you, this is the last time you shall ever be troubled by the man you so much despise.

LUC. You might have made the favour complete, sir, and spared me also this last trouble.

ERAS. Very well, madam, very well, you shall be satisfied. I here break off all acquaintance with you, and break it off for ever, since you wish it; may I lose my life if ever again I desire to converse with you!

LUC. So much the better, you will oblige me.

ERAS. No, no, do not be afraid that I shall break my word! For, though my heart may be weak enough not to be able to efface your image, be assured you shall never have the pleasure of seeing me return.

LUC. You may save yourself the trouble.

ERAS. I would pierce my breast a hundred times should I ever be so mean as to see you again, after this unworthy treatment.

LUC. Be it so; let us talk no more about it.

ERAS. Yes, yes; let us talk no more about it; and to make an end here of all unnecessary speeches, and to give you a convincing proof, ungrateful woman, that I forever throw off your chain, I will keep nothing which may remind me of what I must forget. Here is your portrait; it presents to the eye many wonderful and dazzling charms, but underneath them lurk as many monstrous faults; it is a delusion which I restore to you.

GR.-RE. You are right.

LUC. And I, not to be behind-hand with you in the idea of returning everything, restore to you this diamond which you obliged me to accept.

MAR. Very well.

ERAS. Here is likewise a bracelet of yours.

[Formerly lovers used to wear bracelets generally made of each others hair, which no doubt were hidden from the common view. Shakespeare, in his ***Mid-summer Night's Dream***, Act i, Scene I, says, "Thou, Lysander, thou hast... stol'n th' impression of her fantasy with bracelets of thy hair."]

LUC. And this agate seal is yours.

ERAS. (***Reads***). "You love me with the most ardent passion, Eraste, and wish to know if I feel the same. If I do not love Eraste as much, at least I am pleased that Eraste should thus love me.--LUCILE." You assure me by this letter that you accept my love; it is a falsehood which I punish thus. (***Tears the letter***).

LUC. (***Reading***). "I do not know what may be the fate of my ardent love, nor how long I shall suffer; but this I know, beauteous charmer, that I shall always love you.--ERASTE." This is an assurance of everlasting love; both the hand and the letter told a lie. (Tears the letter).

GR.-RE. Go on.

ERAS. (***Showing another letter***). This is another of your letters; it shall share the same fate.

MAR. (***To Lucile***). Be firm.

LUC. (***Tearing another letter***). I should be sorry to keep back one of them.

GR.-RE. (***To Eraste***). Do not let her have the last word.

MAR. (***To Lucile***). Hold out bravely to the end.

LUC. Well, there are the rest.

ERAS. Thank Heaven, that is all! May I be struck dead if I do not keep my word!

LUC. May it confound me if mine be vain.

ERAS. Farewell, then.

LUC. Farewell, then.

MAR. (*To Lucile*). Nothing could be better.

GR.-RE. (*To Eraste*). You triumph.

MAR. (*To Lucile*). Come, let us leave him.

GR.-RE. (*To Eraste*). You had best retire after this courageous effort.

MAR. (*To Lucile*). What are you waiting for?

GR.-RE. (*To Eraste*). What more do you want?

ERAS. Ah, Lucile, Lucile! you will be sorry to lose a heart like mine, and I know it.

LUC. Eraste, Eraste, I may easily find a heart like yours.

ERAS. No, no, search everywhere; you will never find one so passionately fond of you, I assure you. I do not say this to move you to pity; I should be in the wrong now to wish it; the most respectful passion could not bind you. You wanted to break with me; I must think of you no more.

But whatever any one may pretend, nobody will ever love you so tenderly as I have done.

LUC. When a woman is really beloved she is treated differently, and is not condemned so rashly.

ERAS. Those who love are apt to be jealous on the slightest cause of suspicion, but they can never wish to lose the object of their adoration, and that you have done.

LUC. Pure jealousy is more respectful.

ERAS. An offence caused by love is looked upon with more indulgence.

LUC. No, Eraste, your flame never burnt very bright.

ERAS. No, Lucile, you never loved me.

LUC. Oh! that does not trouble you much, I suppose; perhaps it would have been much better for me if... But no more of this idle talk; I do not say what I think on the subject.

ERAS. Why?

LUC. Because, as we are to break, it would be out of place, it seems to me.

ERAS. Do we break, then?

LUC. Yes, to be sure; have we not done so already?

ERAS. And you can do this calmly?

LUC. Yes; so can you.

ERAS. I?

LUC. Undoubtedly. It is weakness to let people see that we are hurt by losing them.

ERAS. But, hard-hearted woman, it is you who would have it so.

LUC. I? not at all; it was you who took that resolution.

ERAS. I? I thought it would please you.

LUC. Me; not at all; you did it for your own satisfaction.

ERAS. But what if my heart should wish to resume its former chain? If, though very sad, it should sue for pardon...?

[An imitation from Horace, book iii., ode ix., vers. 17 and 18.
  Quid? si prisca redet Venus
  Diductosque jugo cogit aheneo?]

LUC. No, no; do no such thing; my weakness is too great. I am afraid I might too quickly grant your request.

ERAS. Oh! you cannot grant it, nor I ask for it, too soon, after what I have just heard. Consent to love me still, madam; so pure a flame ought to burn for ever, for your own sake. I ask for it, pray grant me this kind pardon.

LUC. Lead me home.

SCENE IV.--MARINETTE, GROS-RENE.

MAR. Oh! cowardly creature,

GR.-RE. Oh! weak courage.

MAR. I blush with indignation.

GR.-RE. I am swelling with rage; do not imagine I will yield thus.

MAR. And do not think to find such a dupe in me.

GR.-RE. Come on, come on; you shall soon see what my wrath is capable of doing.

MAR. I am not the person you take me for; you have not my silly mistress to deal with. It is enough to look at that fine phiz to be smitten with the man himself! Should I fall in love with your beastly face? Should I hunt after you? Upon my word, girls like us are not for the like of you.

GR.-RE. Ay! and you address me in such a fashion? Here, here, without any further compliments, there is your bow of tawdry lace, and your narrow ribbon; it shall not have the honour of being on my ear any more.

MAR. And to show you how I despise you, here, take back your half hundred of Paris pins, which you gave me yesterday with so much bragging.

GR.-RE. Take back your knife too; a thing most rich and rare; it cost you about twopence when you made me a present of it.

MAR. Take back your scissors with the pinchbeck chain.

GR.-RE. I forgot the piece of cheese you gave me the day before yesterday--here it is; I wish I could bring back the broth you made me eat, so that I might have nothing belonging to you.

MAR. I have none of your letters about me now, but I shall burn every one of them.

GR.-RE. And do you know what I shall do with yours?

MAR. Take care you never come begging to me again to forgive you.

GR. RE. (*Picking up a bit of straw*). To cut off every way of being reconciled, we must break this straw between us; when a straw is broken, it settles an affair between people of honour.

[A wisp of straw, or a stick, was formerly used as a symbol of investiture of a feudal fief. According to some authors the breaking of the straw or stick was a proof that the vassals renounced their homage; hence the allusion of Moliere. The breaking of a staff was also typical of the voluntary or compulsory abandonment of power. Formerly, after the death of the kings of France, the *grand maitre* (master of the household) broke his wand of office over the grave, saying aloud three times, *le roi est mort* and then *Vive le roi*. Hence also, most likely, the saying of Prospero, in Shakespeare's "Tempest" Act v. Sc. I, "I'll break my staff," *i.e.*, I voluntarily abandon my power. Sometimes the breaking of a staff betokened dishonour, as in Shakespeare's second part of "Henry VI." Act I. Sc. 2. when Gloster says: "Methought this staff, mine office-badge in court was broke in twain."]

Cast none of your sheep's eyes at me;

[According to tradition, Gros-Rene and Marinette stand on the stage back to back; from time to time they look to the right and to the left; when their looks meet they turn their heads abruptly away, whilst Gros-Rene presents over his shoulder to Marinette the piece of straw, which the latter takes very good care not to touch.]

I will be angry.

MAR. Do not look at me thus; I am too much provoked.

GR.-RE. Here, break this straw; this is the way of never recanting again; break. What do you laugh at, you jade?

MAR. Yes, you make me laugh.

GR.-RE. The deuce take your laughing! all my anger is already softened. What do you say? shall we break or not?

MAR. Just as you please.

GR.-RE. Just as you please.

MAR. Nay, it shall be as you please.

GR. RE. Do you wish me never to love you?

MAR. I? As you like.

GR.-RE. As you yourself like; only say the word.

MAR. I shall say nothing.

GR.-RE. Nor I.

MAR. Nor I.

GR.-RE. Faith! we had better forswear all this nonsense; shake hands, I pardon you.

MAR. And I forgive you.

GR.-RE. Bless me! how you bewitch me with your charms.

MAR. What a fool is Marinette when her Gros-Rene is by.

ACT V.

SCENE I.--MASCARILLE, *alone*.

"As soon as darkness has invaded the town, I will enter Lucile's room; go, therefore, and get ready immediately the dark lantern, and whatever arms are necessary." When my master said these words, it sounded in my ears as if he had said, "Go quickly and get a halter to hang yourself." But come on, master of mine, for I was so astonished when first I heard your order, that I had no time to answer you; but I shall talk with you now, and confound you; therefore defend yourself well, and let us argue without making a noise. You say you wish to go and visit Lucile to-night? "Yes, Mascarille." And what do you propose to do? "What a lover does who wishes to be convinced." What a man does who has very little brains, who risks his carcass when there is no occasion for it. "But do you know what is my motive? Lucile is angry." Well, so much the worse for her. "But my love prompts me to go and appease her." But love is a fool, and does not know what he says: will this same love defend us against an enraged rival, father, or brother? "Do you think any of them intend to harm us?" Yes, really, I do think so; and especially this rival. "Mascarille, in any case, what I trust to is, that we shall go well armed, and if anybody interrupts us we shall draw." Yes, but that is precisely what your servant does not wish to do. I draw! Good Heavens! am I a Roland, master, or a Ferragus?

[Roland, or Orlando in Italian, one of Charlemagne's paladins
and nephew is represented as brave, loyal, and simple-minded. On the
return of Charlemagne from Spain, Roland, who commanded the rearguard,
fell into an ambuscade at Roncezvalles, in the Pyrenees (778), and
perished, with the flower of French chivalry. He is the hero of
Ariosto's poem, "Orlando Furioso." In this same poem Cant. xii. is also
mentioned Ferragus, or Ferrau in Italian, a Saracen giant, who dropped
his helmet into the river, and vowed he would never wear another till he
had won that worn by Orlando; the latter slew him in the only part where
he was vulnerable.]

You hardly know me. When I, who love myself so dearly, consider that two
inches of cold steel in this body would be quite sufficient to send a
poor mortal to his last home, I am particularly disgusted. "But you will
be armed from head to foot." So much the worse. I shall be less nimble
to get into the thicket; besides, there is no armour so well made but
some villainous point will pierce its joints. "Oh! you will then be
considered a coward." Never mind; provided I can but always move my
jaws. At table you may set me down for as good as four persons, if you
like; but when fighting is going on, you must not count me for anything.
Moreover, if the other world possesses charms for you, the air of this
world agrees very well with me. I do not thirst after death and wounds;
if you have a mind to play the fool, you may do it all by yourself, I
assure you.

SCENE II.--VALERE, MASCARILLE.

VAL. I never felt a day pass more slowly; the sun seems to have forgotten himself; he has yet such a course to run before he reaches his bed, that I believe he will never accomplish it; his slow motion drives me mad.

MASC. What an eagerness to go in the dark, to grope about for some ugly adventure! You see that Lucile is obstinate in her repulses....

VAL. A truce to these idle remonstrances. Though I were sure to meet a hundred deaths lying in ambush, yet I feel her wrath so greatly, that I shall either appease it, or end my fate. I am resolved on that.

MASC. I approve of your design; but it is unfortunate, sir, that we must get in secretly.

VAL. Very well.

MASC. And I am afraid I shall only be in the way.

VAL. How so?

MASC. I have a cough which nearly kills me, and the noise it makes may betray you. Every moment... (*He coughs*). You see what a punishment it is.

VAL. You will get better; take some liquorice.

MASC. I do not think, sir, it will get better. I should be delighted to go with you, but I should be very sorry if any misfortune should befall my dear master through me.

SCENE III.--VALERE, LA RAPIERE, MASCARILLE.

LA RA. Sir, I have just now heard from good authority that Eraste is greatly enraged against you, and that Albert talks also of breaking all the bones in Mascarille's body, on his daughter's account.

MASC. I? I have nothing to do with all this confusion. What have I done to have all the bones in my body broken? Am I the guardian of the virginity of all the girls in the town, that I am to be thus threatened? Have I any influence with temptation? Can I help it, I, poor fellow, if I have a mind to try it?

VAL. Oh! they are not so dangerous as they pretend to be; however courageous love may have made Eraste, he will not have so easy a bargain with us.

LA RA. If you should have any need for it, my arm is entirely at your service. You know me to be at all times staunch.

[It is thought the introduction of Mons. de la Rapiere contains an allusion to the poor noblemen of Languedoc, who formerly made a kind of living by being seconds at duels, and whom the Prince de Conti compelled to obey the edicts of Louis XIV. against duelling. *The Love-tiff* was first played in 1656 at Beziers, where the States of Languedoc were assembled.]

VAL. I am much obliged to you, M. de la Rapiere.

LA RA. I have likewise two friends I can procure, who will draw against all comers, and upon whom you may safely rely.

MASC. Accept their services, sir.

VAL. You are too kind.

LA RA. Little Giles might also have assisted us, if a sad accident had not taken him from us. Oh, sir, it is a great pity! He was such a handy fellow, too! You know the trick justice played him; he died like a hero; when the executioner broke him on the wheel, he made his exit without uttering a word.

VAL. M. de la Rapiere, such a man ought to be lamented, but, as for your escort, I thank you, I want them not.

LA RA. Be it so, but do not forget that you are sought after, and may have some scurvy trick played upon you.

VAL. And I, to show you how much I fear him, will offer him the satisfaction he desires, if he seeks me; I will immediately go all over the town, only accompanied by Mascarille.

SCENE IV.--VALERE, MASCARILLE.

MASC. What, sir? will you tempt Heaven? Do not be so presumptuous! Lack-a-day! you see how they threaten us. How on every side...

VAL. What are you looking at yonder?

MASC. I smell a cudgel that way. In short, if you will take my prudent advice, do not let us be so obstinate as to remain in the street; let us go and shut ourselves up.

VAL. Shut ourselves up, rascal? How dare you propose to me such a base action? Come along, and follow me, without any more words.

MASC. Why, sir, my dear master, life is so sweet! One can die but once, and it is for such a long time!

VAL. I shall half kill you, if I hear anything more. Here comes Ascanio; let us leave him; we must find out what side he will choose. However, come along with me into the house, to take whatever arms we may want.

MASC. I have no great itching for fighting. A curse on love and those darned girls, who will be tasting it, and then look as if butter would not melt in their mouth.

SCENE V.--ASCANIO, FROSINE.

ASC. Is it really true, Frosine, do I not dream? Pray tell me all that
has happened, from first to last.

FROS. You shall know all the particulars in good time; be patient; such
adventures are generally told over and over again, and that every
moment. You must know then that after this will, which was on condition
of a male heir being born, Albert's wife who was *enceinte*, gave
birth to you. Albert, who had stealthily and long beforehand laid his
plan, changed you for the son of Inez, the flower-woman, and gave you to
my mother to nurse, saying it was her own child. Some ten months after,
death took away this little innocent, whilst Albert was absent; his wife
being afraid of her husband, and inspired by maternal love, invented a
new stratagem. She secretly took her own daughter back; you received the
name of the boy, who had taken your place, whilst the death of that
pretended son was kept a secret from Albert, who was told that his
daughter had died. Now the mystery of your birth is cleared up, which
your supposed mother had hitherto concealed. She gives certain reasons
for acting in this manner, and may have others to give, for her
interests were not the same as yours. In short, this visit,

[That is the visit of which Frosine speaks, Act iv., Scene I]

from which I expected so little, has proved more serviceable to your
love than could have been imagined. This Inez has given up all claim to
you. As it became necessary to reveal this secret, on account of your
marriage, we two informed your father of it; a letter of his deceased
wife has confirmed all. Pursuing our reasoning yet farther, and being
rather fortunate as well as skilful, we have so cunningly interwoven the
interests of Albert and of Polydore, so gradually unfolded all this

mystery to the latter, that we might not make things appear too terrible to him in the beginning, and, in a word, to tell you all, so prudently led his mind step by step to a reconciliation, that Polydore is now as anxious as your father to legitimize that connection which is to make you happy.

ASC. Ah! Frosine, what happiness you prepare for me. ... What do I, not owe to your fortunate zeal?

FROS. Moreover, the good man is inclined to be merry, and has forbidden us to mention anything of this affair to his son.

SCENE VI.--POLYDORE, ASCANIO, FROSINE.

POL. Come hither, daughter, since I may give you this name now, for I know the secret which this disguise conceals. You have shown so much resolution, ingenuity, and archness in your stratagem, that I forgive you; I think my son will esteem himself happy when he knows that you are the object of his love. You are worth to him more than all the treasures in this world; and I will tell him so. But here he comes: let us divert ourselves with this event. Go and tell all the people to come hither immediately.

ASC. To obey you, sir, shall be the first compliment I pay you.

SCENE VII.--MASCARILLE, POLYDORE, VALERE.

MASC. Misfortunes are often revealed by Heaven: I dreamt last night of pearls unstrung and broken eggs, sir. This dream depresses my spirits.

[In a little book still sold on the quays of Paris, and called *la Cle des Songes*, it is said that to dream of pearls denotes "embarrassed affairs," and of broken eggs, "loss of place and lawsuits."]

VAL. Cowardly rascal!

POL. Valere, an encounter awaits you, wherein all your valour will be necessary: you are to cope with a powerful adversary.

MASC. Will nobody stir to prevent people from cutting each other's throats? As for me, I do not care about it; but if any fatal accident should deprive you of your son, do not lay the blame on me.

POL. No, no; in this case I myself urge him to do what he ought.

MASC. What an unnatural father!

VAL. This sentiment, sir, shows you to be a man of honour; I respect you the more for it. I know I have offended you, I am to blame for having done all this without a father's consent; but however angry you may be with me, Nature always will prevail. You do what is truly honourable, in not believing that I am to be terrified by the threats of Eraste.

POL. They just now frightened me with his threats, but since then things have changed greatly; you will be attacked by a more powerful enemy, without being able to flee from him.

MASC. Is there no way of making it up?

VAL! I flee!--Heaven forbid! And who can this be?

POL. Ascanio.

VAL. Ascanio?

POL. Yes; you shall see him appear presently.

VAL. He, who has pledged his word to serve me!

POL. Yes, it is he who says he has a quarrel with you; he, who is determined to decide the quarrel by single combat, to which he challenges you.

MASC. He is a good fellow: he knows that generous minds do not endanger other people's lives by their quarrels.

POL. He accuses you of deceit. His anger appears to me to have so just a cause, that Albert and I have agreed you should give Ascanio satisfaction for this affront, but publicly, and without any delay, according to the formalities requisite in such a case.

VAL. What! father; and did Lucile obstinately...?

POL. Lucile is to marry Eraste, and blames you too; and the better to prove your story to be false, is resolved to give her hand to Eraste before your very face.

VAL. Ha! this impudence is enough to drive me mad. Has she lost, then, all sense, faith, conscience, and honour?

SCENE VIII.--ALBERT, POLYDORE, LUCILE, ERASTE, VALERE, MASCARILLE.

ALB. Well! where are the combatants? They are bringing ours. Have you prepared yours for the encounter?

VAL. Yes, yes; I am ready, since you compel me to it; if I at all hesitated, it was because I still felt a little respect, and not on account of the valour of the champion who is to oppose me. But I have been urged too far. This respect is at an end; I am prepared for any catastrophe! I have been treated so strangely and treacherously, that my love must and shall be revenged. (*To Lucile*). Not that I still pretend to your hand: my former love is now swallowed up in wrath; and when I have made your shame public, your guilty marriage will not in the least disturb me. Lucile, your behaviour is infamous: scarcely can I believe my own eyes. You show yourself so opposed to all modesty, that you ought to die for shame.

LUC. Such reproaches might affect me, if I had not one at hand to avenge my cause. Here comes Ascanio; he shall soon have the pleasure, and without giving himself much trouble, of making you change your language.

SCENE IX.--ALBERT, POLYDORE, ASCANIO, LUCILE, ERASTE, VALERE, FROSINE, MARINETTE, GROS-RENE, MASCARILLE.

VAL. He shall not make me change my language, though he had twenty arms besides his own. I am sorry he defends a guilty sister; but since he is foolish enough to pick a quarrel with me, I shall give him satisfaction, and you also, my valiant gentleman.

ERAS. A short time ago I took an interest in this, but as Ascanio has taken the affair upon himself, I will have nothing more to do with it, but leave it to him.

VAL. You do well; prudence is always timely, but...

ERAS. He shall give you satisfaction for us all.

VAL. He?

POL. Do not deceive yourself; you do not yet know what a strange fellow Ascanio is.

ALB. He is blind to it now, but Ascanio will let him know in a little time.

VAL. Come on, then; let him do so now.

MAR. What! before everybody?

GR.-RE. That would not be decent.

VAL. Are you making fun of me? I will break the head of any fellow who laughs. But let us see what Ascanio is going to do.

ASC. No, no. I am not so bad as they make me out; in this adventure, in which every one has put me forward, you shall see my weakness appear more than anything else; you will discover that Heaven, to which we must all submit, did not give me a heart to hold out against you, but that it reserved for you the easy triumph of putting an end to Lucile's brother. Yes; far from boasting of the power of his arm, Ascanio shall receive death from your hands; nay, would gladly die, if his death could contribute to your satisfaction, by giving you, in the presence of all this company, a wife who lawfully belongs to you.

VAL. No, even the whole world, after her perfidy and shamelessness...

ASC. Ah! Valere, allow me to tell you that the heart which is pledged to you is guilty of no crime against you; her love is still pure, and her constancy unshaken; I call your own father himself to witness that I speak the truth.

POL. Yes, son, we have laughed enough at your rage; I see it is time to undeceive you; she to whom you are bound by oath is concealed under the dress you here behold. Some question about property was the cause of this disguise, which from her earliest youth deceived so many people. Lately love was the cause of another which deceived you, whilst it made of the two families but one. Yes, in a word, it is she whose subtle skill obtained your hand at night, who pretended to be Lucile, and by this contrivance, which none discovered, has perplexed you all so much. But since Ascanio now gives place to Dorothea, your love must be free from every appearance of deceit, and be strengthened by a more sacred knot!

ALB. This is the single combat by which you were to give us satisfaction for your offence, and which is not forbidden by any laws.

[Severe laws were promulgated in the preceding reign against duelling; Louis XIV. also published two edicts against it in 1643 and in 1651. *The Love-Tiff* was first performed in 1656.]

POL. Such an event amazes you, but all hesitation is now too late.

VAL. No, no, I do not hesitate; if this adventure astonishes me, it is a flattering surprise; I find myself seized with admiration, love, and pleasure. Is it possible that those eyes...?

ALB. This dress, dear Valere, is not a proper one to hear your fine speeches in. Let her go and put on another, and meanwhile you shall know the particulars of the event.

VAL. Pardon me, Lucile, if my mind, duped by...

LUC. It is easy to forget that.

ALB. Come, these compliments will do as well at home; we shall then have plenty of time to pay them to one another.

ERAS. But in talking thus you do not seem to think that there is still occasion for manslaughter here. Our loves are indeed crowned, but who ought to obtain the hand of Marinette, his Mascarille or my Gros-Rene? This affair must end in blood.

MASC. No, no, my blood suits my body too well; let him marry her in peace, it will be nothing to me. I know Marinette too well to think marriage will be any bar to my courting her.

MAR. And do you think I will make my gallant of you? A husband does not matter; anything will do for that. We do not stand, then, upon so much ceremony; but a gallant should be well made enough to make one's mouth water.

GR.-RE. Listen! When we are united by marriage, I insist that you should turn a deaf ear to all sparks.

MASC. Do you think, brother, to marry her for yourself alone?

GR.-RE. Of course; I will have a virtuous wife, or else I shall kick up a fine row.

MASC. Ah! lack-a-day, you shall do as others, and become more gentle. Those people who are so severe and critical before marriage, often degenerate into pacific husbands.

MAR. Make yourself easy, my dear husband, and do not have the least fear about my fidelity; flattery will produce no impression on me, and I shall tell you everything.

MASC. Oh! what a cunning wench to make of a husband a confidant.

MAR. Hold your tongue, you knave of clubs.

[The original has *as de pique*, and different commentators have of course given various explanations. But why, says M. Despois, should Marinette, who appears to be fond of cards, not call people by names derived from her favourite game? She calls Gros-Rene in another place *beau valet de carreau*.]

ALB. For the third time, I say, let us go home, and continue at leisure such an agreeable conversation.

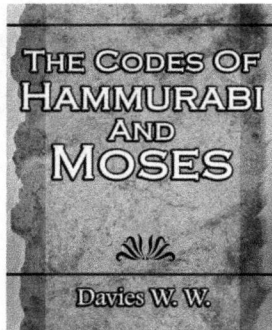

The Codes Of Hammurabi And Moses
W. W. Davies

QTY

The discovery of the Hammurabi Code is one of the greatest achievements of archaeology, and is of paramount interest, not only to the student of the Bible, but also to all those interested in ancient history...

Religion   **ISBN:** *1-59462-338-4*   **Pages:132**

MSRP $12.95

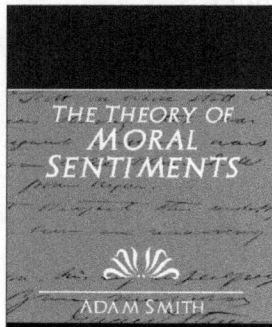

The Theory of Moral Sentiments
Adam Smith

QTY

This work from 1749. contains original theories of conscience amd moral judgment and it is the foundation for systemof morals.

Philosophy   **ISBN:** *1-59462-777-0*   **Pages:536**

MSRP $19.95

Jessica's First Prayer
Hesba Stretton

QTY

In a screened and secluded corner of one of the many railway-bridges which span the streets of London there could be seen a few years ago, from five o'clock every morning until half past eight, a tidily set-out coffee-stall, consisting of a trestle and board, upon which stood two large tin cans, with a small fire of charcoal burning under each so as to keep the coffee boiling during the early hours of the morning when the work-people were thronging into the city on their way to their daily toil...

Pages:84

Childrens   **ISBN:** *1-59462-373-2*   *MSRP $9.95*

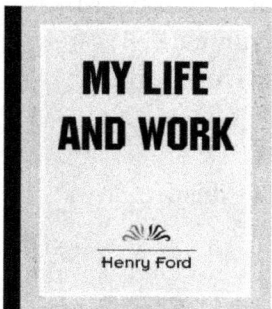

My Life and Work
Henry Ford

QTY

Henry Ford revolutionized the world with his implementation of mass production for the Model T automobile. Gain valuable business insight into his life and work with his own auto-biography... "We have only started on our development of our country we have not as yet, with all our talk of wonderful progress, done more than scratch the surface. The progress has been wonderful enough but..."

Pages:300

Biographies/   **ISBN:** *1-59462-198-5*   *MSRP $21.95*

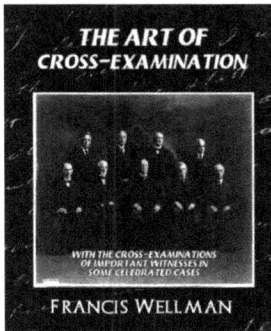

The Art of Cross-Examination
Francis Wellman

QTY

I presume it is the experience of every author, after his first book is published upon an important subject, to be almost overwhelmed with a wealth of ideas and illustrations which could readily have been included in his book, and which to his own mind, at least, seem to make a second edition inevitable. Such certainly was the case with me; and when the first edition had reached its sixth impression in five months, I rejoiced to learn that it seemed to my publishers that the book had met with a sufficiently favorable reception to justify a second and considerably enlarged edition. ..

Pages:412

Reference   ISBN: *1-59462-647-2*   *MSRP $19.95*

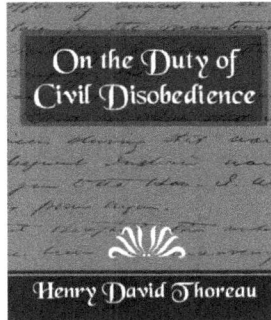

On the Duty of Civil Disobedience
Henry David Thoreau

QTY

Thoreau wrote his famous essay, On the Duty of Civil Disobedience, as a protest against an unjust but popular war and the immoral but popular institution of slave-owning. He did more than write—he declined to pay his taxes, and was hauled off to gaol in consequence. Who can say how much this refusal of his hastened the end of the war and of slavery ?

Law   ISBN: *1-59462-747-9*   **Pages:48**
                                            MSRP $7.45

Dream Psychology Psychoanalysis for Beginners
Sigmund Freud

QTY

Sigmund Freud, born Sigismund Schlomo Freud (May 6, 1856 - September 23, 1939), was a Jewish-Austrian neurologist and psychiatrist who co-founded the psychoanalytic school of psychology. Freud is best known for his theories of the unconscious mind, especially involving the mechanism of repression; his redefinition of sexual desire as mobile and directed towards a wide variety of objects; and his therapeutic techniques, especially his understanding of transference in the therapeutic relationship and the presumed value of dreams as sources of insight into unconscious desires.

Pages:196

Psychology   ISBN: *1-59462-905-6*   *MSRP $15.45*

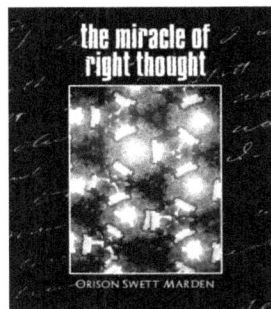

The Miracle of Right Thought
Orison Swett Marden

QTY

Believe with all of your heart that you will do what you were made to do. When the mind has once formed the habit of holding cheerful, happy, prosperous pictures, it will not be easy to form the opposite habit. It does not matter how improbable or how far away this realization may see, or how dark the prospects may be, if we visualize them as best we can, as vividly as possible, hold tenaciously to them and vigorously struggle to attain them, they will gradually become actualized, realized in the life. But a desire, a longing without endeavor, a yearning abandoned or held indifferently will vanish without realization.

Pages:360

Self Help   ISBN: *1-59462-644-8*   *MSRP $25.45*

www.bookjungle.com *email: sales@bookjungle.com fax: 630-214-0564 mail: Book Jungle PO Box 2226 Champaign, IL 61825*

QTY

☐ **The Rosicrucian Cosmo-Conception Mystic Christianity** *by Max Heindel*   ISBN: *1-59462-188-8*   **$38.95**
The Rosicrucian Cosmo-conception is not dogmatic, neither does it appeal to any other authority than the reason of the student. It is: not controversial, but is: sent forth in the, hope that it may help to clear..
New Age/Religion Pages 646

☐ **Abandonment To Divine Providence** *by Jean-Pierre de Caussade*   ISBN: *1-59462-228-0*   **$25.95**
"The Rev. Jean Pierre de Caussade was one of the most remarkable spiritual writers of the Society of Jesus in France in the 18th Century. His death took place at Toulouse in 1751. His works have gone through many editions and have been republished...
Inspirational/Religion Pages 400

☐ **Mental Chemistry** *by Charles Haanel*   ISBN: *1-59462-192-6*   **$23.95**
Mental Chemistry allows the change of material conditions by combining and appropriately utilizing the power of the mind. Much like applied chemistry creates something new and unique out of careful combinations of chemicals the mastery of mental chemistry...
New Age Pages 354

☐ **The Letters of Robert Browning and Elizabeth Barret Barrett 1845-1846 vol II**   ISBN: *1-59462-193-4*   **$35.95**
by Robert Browning and Elizabeth Barrett
Biographies Pages 596

☐ **Gleanings In Genesis (volume I)** *by Arthur W. Pink*   ISBN: *1-59462-130-6*   **$27.45**
Appropriately has Genesis been termed "the seed plot of the Bible" for in it we have, in germ form, almost all of the great doctrines which are afterwards fully developed in the books of Scripture which follow...
Religion/Inspirational Pages 420

☐ **The Master Key** *by L. W. de Laurence*   ISBN: *1-59462-001-6*   **$30.95**
In no branch of human knowledge has there been a more lively increase of the spirit of research during the past few years than in the study of Psychology, Concentration and Mental Discipline. The requests for authentic lessons in Thought Control, Mental Discipline and...
New Age/Business Pages 422

☐ **The Lesser Key Of Solomon Goetia** *by L. W. de Laurence*   ISBN: *1-59462-092-X*   **$9.95**
This translation of the first book of the "Lemegton" which is now for the first time made accessible to students of Talismanic Magic was done, after careful collation and edition, from numerous Ancient Manuscripts in Hebrew, Latin, and French...
New Age/Occult Pages 92

☐ **Rubaiyat Of Omar Khayyam** *by Edward Fitzgerald*   ISBN:*1-59462-332-5*   **$13.95**
Edward Fitzgerald, whom the world has already learned, in spite of his own efforts to remain within the shadow of anonymity, to look upon as one of the rarest poets of the century, was born at Bredfield, in Suffolk, on the 31st of March, 1809. He was the third son of John Purcell...
Music Pages 172

☐ **Ancient Law** *by Henry Maine*   ISBN: *1-59462-128-4*   **$29.95**
The chief object of the following pages is to indicate some of the earliest ideas of mankind, as they are reflected in Ancient Law, and to point out the relation of those ideas to modern thought.
Religion/History Pages 452

☐ **Far-Away Stories** *by William J. Locke*   ISBN: *1-59462-129-2*   **$19.45**
"Good wine needs no bush, but a collection of mixed vintages does. And this book is just such a collection. Some of the stories I do not want to remain buried for ever in the museum files of dead magazine-numbers an author's not unpardonable vanity..."
Fiction Pages 272

☐ **Life of David Crockett** *by David Crockett*   ISBN: *1-59462-250-7*   **$27.45**
"Colonel David Crockett was one of the most remarkable men of the times in which he lived. Born in humble life, but gifted with a strong will, an indomitable courage, and unremitting perseverance...
Biographies/New Age Pages 424

☐ **Lip-Reading** *by Edward Nitchie*   ISBN: *1-59462-206-X*   **$25.95**
Edward B. Nitchie, founder of the New York School for the Hard of Hearing, now the Nitchie School of Lip-Reading, Inc, wrote "LIP-READING Principles and Practice". The development and perfecting of this meritorious work on lip-reading was an undertaking...
How-to Pages 400

☐ **A Handbook of Suggestive Therapeutics, Applied Hypnotism, Psychic Science**   ISBN: *1-59462-214-0*   **$24.95**
by Henry Munro
Health/New Age/Health/Self-help Pages 376

☐ **A Doll's House: and Two Other Plays** *by Henrik Ibsen*   ISBN: *1-59462-112-8*   **$19.95**
Henrik Ibsen created this classic when in revolutionary 1848 Rome. Introducing some striking concepts in playwriting for the realist genre, this play has been studied the world over.
Fiction/Classics/Plays 308

☐ **The Light of Asia** *by sir Edwin Arnold*   ISBN: *1-59462-204-3*   **$13.95**
In this poetic masterpiece, Edwin Arnold describes the life and teachings of Buddha. The man who was to become known as Buddha to the world was born as Prince Gautama of India but he rejected the worldly riches and abandoned the reigns of power when... Religion/History/Biographies Pages 170

☐ **The Complete Works of Guy de Maupassant** *by Guy de Maupassant*   ISBN: *1-59462-157-8*   **$16.95**
"For days and days, nights and nights, I had dreamed of that first kiss which was to consecrate our engagement, and I knew not on what spot I should put my lips..."
Fiction/Classics Pages 240

☐ **The Art of Cross-Examination** *by Francis L. Wellman*   ISBN: *1-59462-309-0*   **$26.95**
Written by a renowned trial lawyer, Wellman imparts his experience and uses case studies to explain how to use psychology to extract desired information through questioning.
How-to/Science/Reference Pages 408

☐ **Answered or Unanswered?** *by Louisa Vaughan*   ISBN: *1-59462-248-5*   **$10.95**
Miracles of Faith in China
Religion Pages 112

☐ **The Edinburgh Lectures on Mental Science (1909)** *by Thomas*   ISBN: *1-59462-008-3*   **$11.95**
This book contains the substance of a course of lectures recently given by the writer in the Queen Street Hall, Edinburgh. Its purpose is to indicate the Natural Principles governing the relation between Mental Action and Material Conditions...
New Age/Psychology Pages 148

☐ **Ayesha** *by H. Rider Haggard*   ISBN: *1-59462-301-5*   **$24.95**
Verily and indeed it is the unexpected that happens! Probably if there was one person upon the earth from whom the Editor of this, and of a certain previous history, did not expect to hear again...
Classics Pages 380

☐ **Ayala's Angel** *by Anthony Trollope*   ISBN: *1-59462-352-X*   **$29.95**
The two girls were both pretty, but Lucy who was twenty-one who supposed to be simple and comparatively unattractive, whereas Ayala was credited, as her Bombwhat romantic name might show, with poetic charm and a taste for romance. Ayala when her father died was nineteen... Fiction Pages 484

☐ **The American Commonwealth** *by James Bryce*   ISBN: *1-59462-286-8*   **$34.45**
An interpretation of American democratic political theory. It examines political mechanics and society from the perspective of Scotsman James Bryce
Politics Pages 572

☐ **Stories of the Pilgrims** *by Margaret P. Pumphrey*   ISBN: *1-59462-116-0*   **$17.95**
This book explores pilgrims religious oppression in England as well as their escape to Holland and eventual crossing to America on the Mayflower, and their early days in New England...
History Pages 268

QTY

The Fasting Cure *by Sinclair Upton*   ISBN: *1-59462-222-1*   **$13.95**
In the Cosmopolitan Magazine for May, 1910, and in the Contemporary Review (London) for April, 1910, I published an article dealing with my experi-
ences in fasting. I have written a great many magazine articles, but never one which attracted so much attention... New Age/Self Help/Health Pages 164

Hebrew Astrology *by Sepharial*   ISBN: *1-59462-308-2*   **$13.45**
In these days of advanced thinking it is a matter of common observation that we have left many of the old landmarks behind and that we are now pressing
forward to greater heights and to a wider horizon than that which represented the mind-content of our progenitors...   Astrology Pages 144

Thought Vibration or The Law of Attraction in the Thought World   ISBN: *1-59462-127-6*   **$12.95**

by William Walker Atkinson   Psychology/Religion Pages 144

Optimism *by Helen Keller*   ISBN: *1-59462-198-X*   **$15.95**
Helen Keller was blind, deaf, and mute since 19 months old, yet famously learned how to overcome these handicaps,
spread her lectures promoting optimism. An inspiring read for everyone...   Biographies/Inspirational Pages 84

Sara Crewe *by Frances Burnett*   ISBN: *1-59462-560-0*   **$9.45**
In the first place, Miss Minchin lived in London. Her home was a large, dull, tall one, in a large, dull square, where all the houses were alike, and all the
sparrows were alike, and where all the door-knockers made the same heavy sound...   Childrens/Classic Pages 88

The Autobiography of Benjamin Franklin *by Benjamin Franklin*   ISBN: *1-59462-135-7*   **$24.95**
The Autobiography of Benjamin Franklin has probably been more extensively read than any other American historical work, and no other book of its kind
has had such ups and downs of fortune. Franklin lived for many years in England, where he was agent...   Biographies/History Pages 332

Name	
Email	
Telephone	
Address	
City, State ZIP	

☐ **Credit Card**   ☐ **Check / Money Order**

Credit Card Number	
Expiration Date	
Signature	

Please Mail to: Book Jungle
PO Box 2226
Champaign, IL 61825
or Fax to: 630-214-0564

ORDERING INFORMATION

web: *www.bookjungle.com*
email: *sales@bookjungle.com*
fax: *630-214-0564*
mail: *Book Jungle PO Box 2226 Champaign, IL 61825*
or PayPal *to sales@bookjungle.com*

Please contact us for bulk discounts

DIRECT-ORDER TERMS

20% Discount if You Order
Two or More Books
Free Domestic Shipping!
Accepted: Master Card, Visa,
Discover, American Express